MARYLAND

IN THE

FRENCH & INDIAN WAR

TIM WARE

THE
History
PRESS

Published by The History Press
Charleston, SC
www.historypress.com

Cherokee Treaty at Fort Frederick, by Bryant White, oil on canvas, 2012.

First published 2023

Manufactured in the United States

ISBN 9781467150347

Library of Congress Control Number: 2022947092

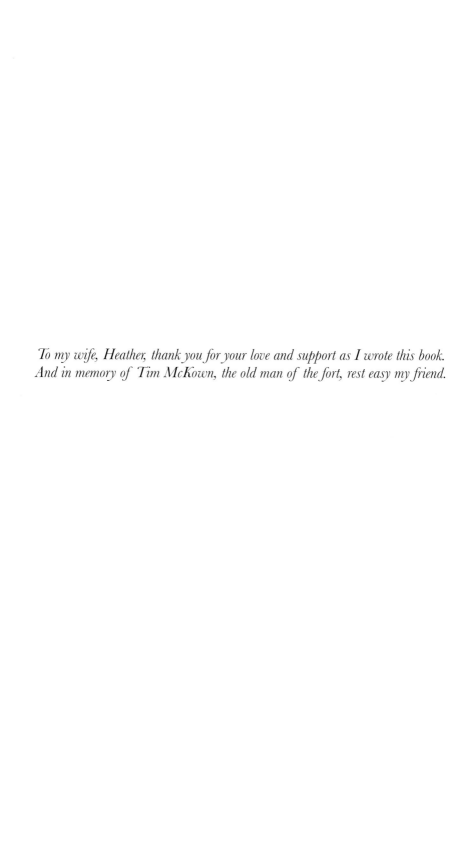

To my wife, Heather, thank you for your love and support as I wrote this book. And in memory of Tim McKown, the old man of the fort, rest easy my friend.

CONTENTS

Introduction   7

1. "Use Your Best Endeavors, to Repeal Force by Force":
   North America on the Eve of War   11

2. "Our Interest in Such an Event…Would Make This Affair Worthy
   or Our Most Serious Consideration": Maryland
   on the Brink of War   22

3. "We Face the Bastions and Curtains with Stone and Shall Mount
   on Each of the Bastions a Six-Pounder":
   Maryland Prepares a Defense   42

4. "The Circumstances of Our Constituents":
   Maryland's Effort Stalls   56

5. "The People of This Province in General Seem Dead to
   All Sense of Gratitude and Duty": Maryland's Inaction   75

6. "But War, Anything, Is Preferable to a Surrender of Our Rights":
   The Road to Revolution   89

Notes   101
Selected Bibliography   115
Index   125
About the Author   128

INTRODUCTION

On November 21, 1754, a colonial officer described Maryland's governor Horatio Sharpe as a "stirring active gentleman... cheerful and free, of good conduct, and one who won't be trifled with."[1] An experienced military officer, Horatio Sharpe had just received a commission giving him command of all colonial forces that were to be arrayed against Fort Duquesne, a French fort that controlled the important river junction where the Allehany and Monongahela Rivers join to form the Ohio River. Whoever controlled that vital river junction controlled a vast domain stretching from western New York to the Mississippi River. Several months before Sharpe's visit to the colonial outpost where the officer was stationed, war had started on the frontiers of North America. This war eventually grew into a global conflict that decided the fates of two European empires in North America.

By 1755, the war was escalating, and Sharpe, understanding the military situation, had to rely on the elected lower house of the Maryland Assembly to lead the colony through the war. Sharpe, however, believed that very little was going to take place, as he "cannot flatter" himself "with any hopes of success."[2] Sharpe would actually be pleasantly surprised when the assembly, at first hesitant to help fellow colonies or plan for the war, passed not one but two funding bills that put Maryland on a wartime footing. Those funding bills paid for Maryland to raise, in essence, its own professional army and construct a massive stone fort that would serve as the backbone

Fort Frederick, built in 1756, today. *Author's collection.*

of the colony's defense from its construction in 1756 to the end of fighting in the region in late 1758. After that early success, however, the relations between Sharpe and the assembly deteriorated as the lower house began to grab for funds and powers that did not belong within the scope of the delegates' duties. By the end of the war, the business of Maryland's colonial government as it pertained to fighting the war had ground to a halt. Despite the gridlock in the colonial government, the citizens of Maryland stepped up, either through the troops raised by the colony or the county militias, to defend Maryland and to bring the war to a successful conclusion that was favorable to British interests.

The French and Indian War changed the face of North America forever. The war itself expanded the domain of Great Britain to include Canada and much of what is now the midwestern United States. The war was incredibly expensive for Great Britain, and the expansion of its empire in America required further spending. To pay for it, the American colonists were taxed on several occasions. These taxes caused nearly a decade of protests that, at times, turned violent. These protests and the ensuing treatment of the colonies by Great Britain eventually led to open conflict in the American Revolution. The purpose of this study is to create an updated interpretation of Maryland's role in the French and Indian War and to show how the colony handled the postwar years leading up to the Revolution. Horatio Sharpe, a military officer turned politician, struggled to focus the colony's efforts while the elected delegates of the Maryland Assembly, in an effort to throw off the proprietorship of the Calvert family, became increasingly uninterested in supporting the war unless its preferred funding methods were used. This political struggle had dire consequences for those living in Maryland. The quotes used within this study may appear to contain spelling and grammatical errors. However, they are presented exactly as they were originally written.

1

"USE YOUR BEST ENDEAVORS, TO REPEAL FORCE BY FORCE"

NORTH AMERICA ON THE EVE OF WAR

I n the early morning hours of August 10, 1753, the sails of a long-awaited ship were spotted on the horizon from the docks of Annapolis, Maryland. This ship, the *Molly*, captained by Nicholas Coxen, was carrying an important passenger. On board was Maryland's newly appointed colonial governor Horatio Sharpe.[3] It would be several more hours before Sharpe disembarked. Awaiting him at the docks was a delegation of Maryland's political leadership, primarily members of the governor's council, who escorted Sharpe to various functions before taking him to the colony's statehouse. There he officially took on his role as Maryland's governor. He issued a proclamation declaring his new role, "notifying…all officers, both civil and military, [to] execute and discharge the…duties in them reposed and enjoined…until such time as my further pleasure and directions shall be signified therein."[4] Sharpe's duties encompassed not only civilian endeavors but also those of the military. Settling into his new position, Sharpe and Maryland were tested by a war that had been brewing since the first European settlers arrived on the shores of North America.

Since the arrival of the first explorers in the North America, the availability of new lands and seemingly endless natural resources provided an opportunity to expand the wealth and power of the respective European powers. In North America, vast swaths of land were claimed by England, France and Spain. The first permanent settlements established by England at Jamestown (1607) and Plymouth (1620) and France at Quebec (1609) set the stage for their respective empires to grow.[5] By the start of the eighteenth century, the French claimed a land mass that covered nearly half the continent, stretching from the St. Lawrence River and Great Lakes in the north to the mouth of the Mississippi River on the Gulf of Mexico. Their claims to these lands were possible because the French claimed not only the land touched by major rivers like the Alleghany and Ohio Rivers but also lands touched by the tributaries of those rivers. These claims ultimately created points of conflict with English settlers, particularly in the western lands claimed respectively by the colonies of New York, Pennsylvania and Virginia. Another European power, Spain, claimed vast amounts of land in the western

HORATIO SHARPE
Governor of Maryland.

Maryland's colonial governor Horatio Sharpe. *From the New York Public Library.*

reaches of the continent, as well as lands east of French Louisiana that ran along the Gulf Coast. With the French and Spanish laying claim to the majority of North America, England (later Great Britain following the unification of England and Scotland under the 1706 Treaty of Union) was largely confined to land along the Atlantic coast in the east. The western expansion of these colonies was limited by the Appalachian Mountains and the French beyond. Despite the size of the North American continent and the relative isolation of the respective European colonies, the inevitable growth, particularly of the English colonies, made open conflict between the major powers almost certain. The inevitability of this conflict in North America, especially between Great Britain and France, can be seen in the major wars of Europe bleeding over into smaller colonial fights in North America, like King William's War (called the War of the League of Augsburg in Europe, 1688–97) and Queen Anne's War (called the War of Spanish Succession, 1702–13, in Europe).[6] While Europeans settled in North America and European wars spilled over into their North American colonies, the colonists' actions had incredible impacts on the Native population of North America that forced them to choose sides.

For thousands of years, North America's Native population thrived. Of course, conflict was ever present between the respective tribes of the

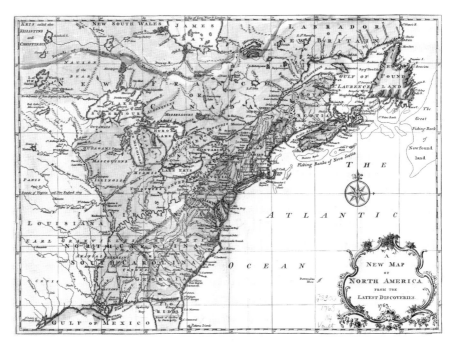

A new map of North America showing French and British possessions in 1763. *Library of Congress, Geography and Map Division.*

continent, as they each developed their own distinct cultural and societal groups. Despite this conflict, Natives were able to, more or less, move about the continent freely, taking advantage of its abundant resources. By the time of first European contact, the population of North American was estimated to be in the millions.[7] After the arrival of Europeans on the shores of North America, the Native populations begin to suffer. In eastern North America, in the lands settled by the French and English, this arrival introduced a new, much more deadly component to the daily lives of the Native population: for the first time, this population was exposed to deadly diseases like smallpox and measles. This exposure decimated the population. At the outbreak of the French and Indian War in the 1750s, a population that once stood in the millions now numbered only a few hundred thousand.[8] This decline in the population influenced the relationship between each Native tribe and the respective European enclaves.

Once their settlements were firmly established, the French and English begin to facilitate relationships with the Natives in an attempt to avoid conflict and promote trade. During the early years of settlement, the Native population loss from disease caused tribes to open trade with Europeans for military goods (weapons, ammunition, et cetera) that would assist them in fighting what were known as mourning wars.[9] These wars took place as attempts for one tribe to replace members who had died due to disease or conflict. In fighting this kind of war, Natives captured women and children from opposing tribes and assimilated them into their own tribal culture. The most successful group in conducting this type of warfare was the Iroquois, a collection of tribes with similar religious and ceremonial traditions. They were so successful, in fact, that by the late seventeenth century, the Iroquois controlled large swaths of eastern North America, including western New York, the Ohio Valley, the Great Lakes Region and even into the backcountry of the Carolinas.[10] With the expansion of territory controlled by the Iroquois, Native tribes, like the Delaware in Pennsylvania, continued to reside on the land but were not official members of the Iroquois Confederacy. These tribes were allowed to retain their independence as distinct tribes, but the Iroquois controlled them by issuing directives, handling treaty negotiations with Europeans and demanding that tributes be paid in the form of European trade goods.[11] One example of the influence wielded by the Iroquois was the forceful movement of the Delaware after they were pushed off their ancestral lands along the lower Delaware River. Settling on land claimed by the Iroquois, the Delaware were again forced from their homes during the infamous Walking Purchase of 1737. Losing a substantial portion of their lands, the Delaware, under pressure from the Iroquois and English settlers, moved further west into the Susquehanna Valley. The Delaware would be forced from their lands twice more before eventually heading westward to the Ohio country in the early 1750s.[12] This consistent pressure to move westward would play a role in the coming conflict. Using this influence, the Iroquois were in a prime position to play the rival European empires against each other.

   As the European colonies in North America grew and conflicts in Europe spread to these colonies, the Iroquois found themselves acting as a sort of buffer zone between the French in Canada and English along the eastern seaboard. They even formed various alliances built largely around the extremely lucrative fur trade. European traders would seek out furs, and in return, the Natives would receive military and other trade goods from the Europeans. In times of war, the alliances forged through this fur trade played a critical role. Not wanting to sacrifice trade, the Iroquois took a relatively weak position of neutrality when France and England went to war. Despite this proclamation of neutrality, warriors from the various Iroquois tribes found themselves taking sides during the colonial conflicts that occurred in the late 1600s and into the first half of the 1700s. The English tended to gain support, both militarily and economically, from the Iroquois tribes of New York, while the French found support in those tribes located around the Great Lakes Region.[13] In these wars, the French learned that Native raids along the English frontier settlements could sow terror among the populace and allow French possessions to remain incredibly defensible. On the other hand, the English, while working to build a relationship with the Native population, failed to take advantage of the Natives' experience in woodland warfare. This failure led to their ineffective use of the Native population during major conflicts, resulting in a decided French advantage when it came to the level of success experienced during these colonial conflicts. During the War of Austrian Succession (1740–48), called King George's War in the colonies, provincial soldiers from New England captured the seemingly impregnable Fortress Louisburg in the summer of 1745.[14] Despite this success, the negotiated peace that ended the war returned Fortress Louisburg to France in exchange for captured English possessions elsewhere. The exchange left the colonists who had captured the fort furious, and despite Europe being at peace, tensions in North America only continued to rise as the leadership of the European colonies turned their attention toward the junction of two rivers, the Monongahela and Alleghany, where they merge to form the Ohio River. Whoever controlled this junction controlled the interior of eastern North America.

At the conclusion of hostilities in 1748, the focus of French and English colonial leaders shifted to the Ohio River Valley that drains into what is today western Pennsylvania, western New York and the Midwest before flowing into the Mississippi River and eventually the Gulf of Mexico. This river valley was incredibly fertile, and most importantly, the Native population there provided ever-increasing opportunities for commerce. The tribes in this area included the Delaware, Mingo, Wyandotte, Ottawa and those associated with the Iroquois. Each one presented an opportunity to increase trade and European influence, especially from the English perspective, in the region.[15] The upper Ohio River Valley was teeming with wildlife that could provide a boost to the fur trade. It was a region controlled by the Iroquois and under French claim. Despite the French claim, the region was eyed by intrepid English settlers and traders who saw the chance to create better, more prosperous lives than those they had in the more established areas along the East Coast and east of the Appalachian Mountains. The Ohio country, as it was called, could provide

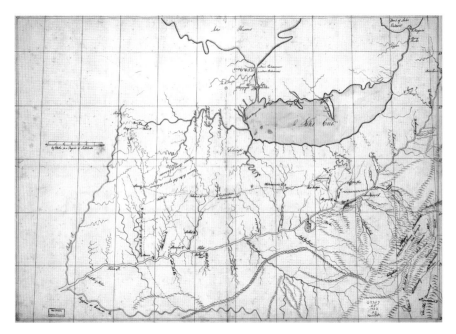

A trader's map of Ohio (1753) showing trade routes and trading post. *Library of Congress, Geography and Map Division.*

ample land for English settlers moving westward from the increasingly crowded coastal areas. Traders, like Pennsylvanian George Croghan, also viewed the area as a means to enrich themselves.[16] The encroachments of English settlers and traders toward lands claimed by the French did sit well with French leadership in New France.

In 1749, just a year after the end of King George's War, New France's governor the Marquis de la Galissoniére ordered Captain Pierre-Joseph Céloron de Blainville to assert, once again, French claims to the Upper Ohio Valley.[17] Departing from Montreal, Céloron's expedition traveled through the Ohio country, restating French claims to the land and planting lead plates at the mouth of each tributary of the Ohio River. Those lead plates renewed French claims by pronouncing "possession…of the said river of Ohio, and of all those which fall into it, and of all those territories on both sides as far as the source of the said rivers."[18] The French were again announcing to the world, especially the encroaching English, that the Ohio River, its tributaries and all the lands that are touched by its waters belonged to France. This encompassed a region that stretches from the headwaters of the Alleghany River in north-central Pennsylvania and western New York to the Ohio River's junction with the Mississippi River.

Céloron's expedition through the Ohio Valley also served a second purpose: it was a show of force by France. Marching with Céloron was a force of 265 *troupe de la marine* (regular French-Canadian infantry) and Native allies.[19] On two separate occasions, Céloron's expedition interacted with English traders. In both instances, the French captain verbally reinforced French claims to the land, advising the English traders that they were illegally trading on lands claimed by the French. In one of the encounters, Céloron wrote of coming upon "six English soldiers, with fifty horses and about one hundred and fifty bales of furs, who were returning from there to Philadelphia."[20] The French captain wrote a summons that was to be delivered to Governor James Hamilton of Pennsylvania. In it, he wrote that he had been sent into the Ohio country in an attempt to renew French friendship with the Natives of the area and was "very surprised to find some merchants of your government in this country, to which England has never had any pretensions."[21] Céloron wrote intentionally that he treated the English with care, as the last war between France and Great Britain had only just recently ended, and he wrote a very clear warning:

> *I hope, Sir, you will...forbid this trade for the future, which is contrary to the treaties; and that you will warn your traders not to return into these territories; for if so, they can only impute to themselves the evils which might befall them. I know that our Governor-General would be very sorry to have to resort to violent measures, but he has received positive orders not to allow foreign merchants or traders in his government.*[22]

The message was clear: any further incursions onto French lands by the English would result in severe repercussions and maybe even violence. Despite the warning, Céloron would acknowledge that even after reasserting French claims and making attempts to renew relationships with the tribes of the Ohio country, "the nations of these countries are ill disposed toward the French and entirely devoted to the English."[23]

Despite the show of force by the French in the Ohio Valley, little was done to dissuade the English from forcing the issue. Following the establishment of the English colonies, the charters clearly laid out southern and northern boundaries, with some disputes taking place between the colonies over the actual boundaries. However, the western boundaries of the colonies were hardly set in stone, and several will lay claim to the Ohio Valley. The colonies situated to benefit the most from westward expansion into the area by English settlers and traders were Virginia and Pennsylvania. Each colony already had trade networks established in the region, as evidenced by the forceful removal of the Pennsylvanian traders by Céloron during his expedition. However, between the two colonies, the most aggressive and persistent was Virginia.

In the latter half of the 1740s, the Virginia Council issued land grants to speculators, opening upward of two million acres of Virginia's western land claims, including the Ohio Valley.[24] While Virginia's colonial government issued land grants, another group was formed to cement not only Virginia's claims to the Ohio but also England's. The Ohio Company of Virginia, otherwise known as the Ohio Company, formed in 1747 after several prominent Virginians petitioned and received a nearly two-hundred-thousand-acre land grant from King George II in the Ohio Country.[25] The grant did come with a stipulation, however. The Ohio Company had to settle two hundred families and erect a fortification to protect the new settlements. With the grant in hand, the Ohio Company began to survey the lands that Captain Céloron's expedition had reinforced French claims to.

In 1750, the Ohio Company hired Christopher Gist, an experienced frontiersman and scout, to explore and survey the massive land grant in the Ohio Valley.[26] Gist received instructions that he was to "go out as soon as possible to the Westward of the great mountains…in Order to search out and discover lands upon the River Ohio & other adjoining branches of the Mississippi down as low as the great Falls."[27] This area that was to be surveyed stretched from the forks of the Ohio River (the location of present-day Pittsburgh, Pennsylvania) to the Great Falls of the Ohio River (near present-day Louisville, Kentucky), and the surrounding areas covered by the tributaries of the Ohio River. The company's effort was very similar to that of the expedition carried out by Captain Céloron. In addition to exploring the land, Gist was also to seek the friendship of the various Native tribes he was likely to encounter. The Ohio Company's instructions wished for Gist to "observe what Nations of Indians inhabit there, their strength & numbers, who they trade with, & what Commodities they deal."[28] Gist began his exploration in October 1750. Over the next several months, he explored the Ohio country, visiting with various Native tribes, including the Shawnee, Delaware, Ottawa, Wyandot, Miami and Mingoe, keeping a journal detailing his interactions with the Native population while also pointing out the suitability of the location for settlement. Completing his exploration in late spring 1751, Gist delivered his journal to the Ohio Company. After studying the journal, the company instructed Gist to again explore the land grant, specifically those areas along the southern end of the Ohio River, with the purpose of finding suitable land for settlement with the additional instruction to "look out & observe the nearest & most convenient Road you can find from the company's storehouse at Will's Creek to a landing at Monongahela."[29] This additional exploration convinced the Ohio Company that any new settlements, for the time being, should be closer to Virginia and located between the company's storehouse at Will's Creek (present-day Cumberland, Maryland) and the confluence of the Alleghany and Monongahela Rivers. The purpose of Gist's exploration for a convenient road west to the forks of the Ohio River served to advance the Ohio Company's intention to build a fort on the forks of the Ohio River and thereby seize control of the Ohio Valley.[30]

The exploration of the Ohio country by Gist also led to a June 1752 conference at Logstown, a Native village in the Ohio Valley. At this meeting, representatives of the Ohio Company pressured the Iroquois into affirming the 1744 Treaty of Lancaster, in which the Iroquois had surrendered land claims west of the Appalachians to Virginia. The Iroquois, mistakenly, believed they had only surrendered land in what is today the Shenandoah Valley. However, in this 1744 treaty, they had surrendered to Virginia all claims to western lands, including the Ohio Valley.[31] Using Virginia's charter and their own interpretation of the Treaty of Lancaster, the Ohio Company forced the Iroquois chieftains who were present to consent to English settlement of the Ohio Valley. With the Ohio Valley now open to English settlement, new issues begin to arise. While the representatives of the Iroquois and Ohio Company met at Logstown, two important tribes living in the area, the Delaware and Shawnee, were excluded from the conference. The exclusion of these two tribes, who were already forced from their ancestral lands in the east, proved to be costly.[32]

While the Ohio Company was busily preparing for settlement of the Ohio Valley, the French were active as well. Knowing the English were continuing their westward movement, the French and their Native allies began a systematic campaign through the upper reaches of the Ohio Valley, attacking and driving away Native tribes who were sympathetic to the English. The campaign even went as far as attacking the English trading posts at Pickawilliny, opening the way for an even larger French effort into the Ohio Valley. Those tribes who were facing the French campaign looked to English colonists to come to their defense. However, those calls for help only resulted in words instead of action from the colonial governments in Virginia and Pennsylvania. This lack of support caused many of these tribes, who were previously very supportive of the English, to realign themselves with the French.[33] With the success of the campaign pressing the English and their allied Natives east and the friendship with Ohio Natives improving, a showdown between the French and English was inevitable. To add to the rising tensions, the French, now commanded by the Marquis Duquesne, Sieur de Menneville, moved to make the French claims to the Ohio Valley more permanent than they had been after simply planting lead plates and writing letters. In the summer of 1753, Duquesne oversaw the construction of a string of forts at Presque Isle, Le Beouf and Venango, creating a support system for a much larger fort to be constructed at the Forks of the Ohio.[34] With the Ohio Company pressing westward from Virginia and the French descending from Canada, tensions were never higher in North America. Whoever gained a foothold at the junction of the Alleghany and Monongahela Rivers in western Pennsylvania could control the continent. Then came a young, ambitious Virginian looking to make a name for himself.

As the summer of 1753 began to wind down, news of the French moving in force into the Ohio Valley arrived in Williamsburg, Virginia, the capital of the colony. Keeping an eye on developments in the Ohio country, Governor Robert Dinwiddie routinely sent dispatches to officials in the royal government reporting on French actions. In response, the English government sent orders to each colonial governor to "use your best endeavors, to repeal Force by Force" but to not appear as the aggressor; those forces were to be used only within the borders of English land claims.[35] Dinwiddie, due to a legislative standoff, could not count on military action. Instead, he sent an envoy carrying a message demanding the French to vacate the Ohio country. To carry his message, Dinwiddie chose a young Virginia militia officer named George Washington.[36] With the assistance of Christopher Gist, arguably the man with the most knowledge of the Ohio country, Washington began his journey west on the first day of November 1753. Just over a month later, Washington, Gist and a collection of fur traders and allied Natives arrived at the French fort at Venango. Unfortunately, the French commander was not in a position to read the letter Washington was to deliver. After a cordial dinner, the following morning, Washington's group continued to Fort Le Beouf with Dinwiddie's message.[37]

Arriving at the French fort, Washington delivered his message to the French commander. Dinwiddie's letter reminded the French that "the lands upon the Ohio in the western parts of the colony of Virginia are… known to be the property of the Crown of Great Britain that is a matter of equal concern and surprise to me to hear that a body of French forces are erecting a fortress and making settlements upon that river [His Majesty's] dominions."[38] Dinwiddie was, despite French claims, calling the French invaders on English soil and was politely yet forcefully requesting them to leave. Washington had to wait three days for a reply. When the French response was received, only open conflict could resolve the issue. The French commander at Le Beouf, Captain Legarduer de Saint-Pierre, responded to Dinwiddie remarking that he wished Washington could have delivered the letter directly to the Marquis Duquense, who could have provided the appropriate evidence proving French claims to the land. Despite this wish, the French commander went on to say, "I do not think myself obliged to obey it....I am here by virtue of the orders of my General and I entreat you, Sir, not to doubt one moment that I am determined to conform myself to them with all exactness and resolution which can be expected from the best of officers."[39] The letter was a challenge. If Virginia and England wanted the Ohio, the French were prepared to fight for it.

By the end of 1753, tensions between England and France in North America were sky high. In Maryland, Horatio Sharpe had only been on duty as governor of the colony for a matter of days before he received instructions from the royal government to prepare military forces to expel a French invasion on the colonial frontier. Over the next several months, various colonial governors, including Robert Dinwiddie (Virginia), William Shirley (Massachusetts) and James De Lancey (New York), were in correspondence with Sharpe, expressing their support for each other in the coming conflict. While events on the Ohio swelled like a flooding river, Sharpe's first order of business was to settle a border dispute between Maryland and Pennsylvania and determine the ownership of the headwaters of the Potomac River. As 1754 dawned, however, Sharpe was unable to avoid the brewing conflict. In January, Governor Dinwiddie wrote to Sharpe that the "progress of the French and their avowed designs make it necessary for me to apply for your assistance and that the men you can furnish may join our people as early as possible in March, at a place called Will's Creek...which I have chosen...believing it to be most convenient to all the Colonies...near the scene of Action. The French have fortified themselves."[40] In office for less than six months, Horatio Sharpe was going to find himself leading Maryland into a war that would determine which European power controlled eastern North America.

2

"OUR INTEREST IN SUCH AN EVENT...

WOULD MAKE THIS AFFAIR WORTHY OF

OUR MOST SERIOUS CONSIDERATION"

MARYLAND ON THE BRINK OF WAR

The end of 1753 saw the French and English (hereafter referred to as British, following the unification of Scotland and England as the Kingdom of Great Britain in 1707) colonies on the brink of war. The construction of a string of forts in the upper Ohio River Valley by the French clearly showed that they would violently respond to further incursions into the area by British traders and settlers. Virginia's message demanding the French to leave the Ohio only added to the tensions. With message in hand, Virginia's envoy George Washington delivered the French response to Robert Dinwiddie, Virginia's governor. In their response, the French refused to leave the Ohio Valley and made it clear that if Virginia wanted the Ohio country, Dinwiddie would have to force the French out. With this ultimatum in hand, Dinwiddie sent for assistance from his neighboring colonies. In Maryland, Horatio Sharpe received the call and prepared to take it before the Maryland Assembly, setting the stage for years of bitter debate as Maryland became involved in the coming war.

To understand the relationship between Maryland's colonial governor and the Maryland Assembly, one must understand how Maryland's colonial government evolved from its founding in the 1630s to the 1750s. The colony that would become known as Maryland, so named by King Charles, began in June 1632, when the efforts of George Calvert come to fruition and his son Cecilius Calvert, the second Lord Baltimore, received a charter to establish a proprietary colony in the new world.[41] As proprietor, Calvert would have had his own fiefdom from which he could enrich himself with a small payment made to the king for that right. The first settlement in the colony was founded when two ships, the *Ark* and the *Dove*, arrived in the Chesapeake Bay in March 1734, and within days, this first settlement, St. Mary's City, was established. Within a year of the arrival of the *Ark* and the *Dove* on the shores of what became Maryland, a collection of colonists gathered to convene Maryland's first colonial assembly. This first gathering, because of the participants' firsthand knowledge of the issues within the new colony, enacted several laws and ordinances according to a section of the land grant provided to Cecilius Calvert. As the proprietor, Calvert will take a much different stance according to his own views of his powers within the land grant. Section 8 of the land grant provided Calvert with the power to propose and enact laws as proprietor of the colony, while the assembly was only a bystander that could make few changes.[42] The assembly interpreted this section as one that gave them the ability to enact and pass laws in place of the proprietor while in session. However, the section also states the proprietor could enact new laws and ordinances when "sudden accidents" happen "before the freeholders of the said province, their delegates, or deputies, can be called together for the framing of laws."[43] The ensuing conflict over legislative power resulted in a compromise in 1638, which allowed the proprietor (Calvert) and elected officials (the assembly) to introduce, debate and pass legislation.[44] By 1650, the assembly had become a bicameral legislative body at the request of the elected members, with the upper house composed of members appointed by the proprietor himself and the lower house comprising members elected by citizens of the colony.[45] These early years of the Maryland Assembly influenced the relationship that later proprietors and their appointed governors, including Horatio Sharpe, had with the elected members of the assembly.

For a period, from the late 1600s to about 1715, the control of Maryland fell under control of an appointed royal governor, due to religious strife that was taking place within the colony. It was during this time the assembly, specifically the elected lower house, took control of several important governmental tasks, creating committees for elections, the passage of laws, the examination of petitions from the populace and, most importantly, looking into the finances of the colony.[46] These simple but extraordinary steps gave the lower house oversight and input into how the colonial government operated, especially when it came to the power of the purse. Within this arrangement, the assembly showed

The Founding of Maryland: Landing at St. Mary's, 1634, by Henry Sadham (1894). *Wallach Division Picture Collection, the New York Public Library.*

that it could willfully and successfully govern the colony as a legislative assembly. Once the proprietorship was reinstated, the assembly managed to retain its new duties and used them to increasingly attack and challenge proprietary rule. By the 1740s, the lower house regularly attacked the finances of the proprietor, taking on itself the need to defend the rights of its constituents.[47] It was this mindset that met Governor Sharpe in the fall of 1753 as he approached the assembly with news of the impending frontier conflict and the need to assist fellow colonies.

The first session of the Maryland Assembly that Sharpe oversaw took place just two months after his arrival in August. In his position, Sharpe had the power to call the assembly into session as he saw fit, and he first called the assembly into session on October 2, 1753. During this session, Sharpe and members of the assembly negotiated and proposed various pieces of legislation. Just like prior sessions before Sharpe's appointment as governor, the lower house of the assembly proposed numerous bills associated with how the colony was funded. One particular bill dealt with the licensing for hawkers and peddlers, similar to business licenses today. The elected lower house wished to use the money gathered from the licensing fees and penalties to pay for county schools within the colony.[48] Unfortunately, the upper house, known as the governor's council, could not approve such a bill. In his position as governor, Horatio Sharpe acted on behalf of the lord proprietor Frederick Calvert and served as his voice in the upper house, a body appointed by Calvert himself. In this position, Sharpe and the upper

Conjectural drawing of the second Maryland Statehouse by Elizabeth Ridout. *Collection of the Maryland State Archives.*

house acted just as the first provincial governor of Maryland was advised by Cecilius Calvert: "You are but merely instrumental in those things to do what I direct."[49] The upper house amended this funding bill, stating that the funds "are the undoubted right of his lordship, the Lord Proprietary, for the support of government."[50] Essentially, the upper house argued that the funds being raised by the proposed bill, due to how they were raised, were to go directly to the proprietor to do with as he wished. This particular bill failed with members of the lower house, who replied with a sharp rebuke, stating that funds taken from the colony by the proprietor, with the exception of the governor's salary, were rarely used to support any government initiatives in Maryland.[51] This back and forth serves as only a preview of what was to come.

During this first session, Sharpe received the letter from Robert Darcy, Lord Holdernesse, that ordered each of the colonial governors in North America to prepare their respective colonies for any French encroachments. The August 1753 letter told the governors to be aware of any transgressions against any "parts of this Majesties Dominions," immediately require them to "desist from any such…undertaking," and, if needs be, call out their own armed forces to "repel force by force."[52] After examining the letter, Sharpe immediately sent a message to the lower house. In his message, Sharpe relayed the urgency of the matter:

> *Our interest in such an event…would make this Affair worthy our most serious consideration. But when you see by that letter…that should the neighboring Colonies make Application to use for assistance, I might be under a necessity of convening you, without respect to the inclemency of the season, or other inconvenience, unless before the conclusion of this session, a fund be established for uses.*[53]

Sharpe expressed his understanding that this funding request may be difficult to fulfill. However, there was no choice. Sharpe requested the revival of the 1704 Law for Arms and Ammunition that put Maryland on a wartime footing. Without this law, Sharpe warned that Maryland would be "unable to defend our private properties, much less…join the neighbouring Colonies…by repelling the Violence of any Enemy."[54]

Sharpe's message was read before the assembly on November 5, 1753, and it took nearly two weeks for the governor to receive a reply. The lower house assured the governor that it was determined to "repel, in the best manner we can, all hostile invasions of this Province, by any foreign power" and come to the assistance of the neighboring colonies as it was able.[55] Despite this assurance, the delegates were unwilling to impose a tax that would raise funds for any assistance Maryland could provide, due to their belief that this was not in the best interest of their constituents. The delegates outright rejected Sharpe's request to revive the 1704 Arms and Ammunition Law. According to the delegates, the law was null and void due to its passage in 1704, while the colony was under the direct protection of the British Crown.[56] In rejecting Sharpe's proposal, the delegates reminded Sharpe that there was a tax of twelve pence per hogshead on tobacco exported out of the colony and that this was collected and paid to the proprietor. From the implementation of this tax, a portion, about one-third, went toward the acquisition of arms and ammunition for the defense of the colony. It was the view of the delegates that the since the tax was still in effect, Sharpe had funds available to answer whatever needs would arise. With the assembly steadfastly denying Sharpe, the governor lamented to the proprietor Frederick Calvert, Lord Baltimore, that "neither the exhortations nor the Secretary of State's letter requiring them to join in the defence [*sic*] of the neighbouring colonies against any hostile attempts of the French or Indians could induce them to think such a timely provision reasonable [and] necessary."[57] Despite the setback, events elsewhere caused the assembly to reconsider Sharpe's request.

Just a week after the Maryland assembly's brief session ended, Governor Robert Dinwiddie of Virginia wrote a letter to Governor Sharpe notifying him that he had been ordered by the Earl of Holderness to send a messenger to the French in the Ohio country.[58] In this same letter, Dinwiddie invited Sharpe to a meeting with Native allies to "make up some breaches… between them [and] endeavor to make peace among themselves" while also ensuring that an alliance was formed between the "several different Nations of Indians…the Crown of Great Britain, [and] the Subjects settled on this continent."[59] Sharpe's military reputation as a former British officer preceded him, and Dinwiddie was hoping to rely on him to help shore up the military situation on the frontiers of Virginia and Maryland.

Dinwiddie's messenger to the French, George Washington, arrived back in Williamsburg in mid-January 1754 with the reply from the French.[60] Reporting the French inclination to not oblige the governor's request and, once again, stating the French claim on the Ohio country, Governor Dinwiddie went before Virginia's general assembly in February to announce Washington's findings. Dinwiddie reported that the French were preparing to continue the construction of forts in the Ohio Valley with a force of at least 1,500 French regulars, along with the Native allies. With some exaggeration, Dinwiddie painted a dim picture of what was happening on the frontier, ending with a plea from the assembly to pass a "full and sufficient Supply to exert the most vigorous efforts…to drive these cruel and treacherous Invadors [sic] of your Properties, and Destroyers of your families."[61]

Following the close of the Maryland Assembly's session in mid-November, Governor Sharpe continued his work settling the official boundaries of the colony, as there were still some disputes with Pennsylvania and Virginia. Sharpe also continued correspondence with his fellow colonial governors regarding mutual assistance should the French press the issue on the frontiers. The governor also surely saw the December 6 issue of the *Maryland Gazette*, in which Dinwiddie's November 1 opening address to the General Assembly of Virginia, detailing French actions in the Ohio Valley, was published. In particular, Dinwiddie told the assembly that information was received from frontier settlements and "neighbouring Governors, of a large Body of French regulars, and Indians in their interest, having marched from Canada to the River Ohio, in an hostile manner, to invade His Majesty's Territories, and having actually built a fort on his Majesty's Land."[62] Despite these words from Dinwiddie, Sharpe seemed unconcerned with the issues

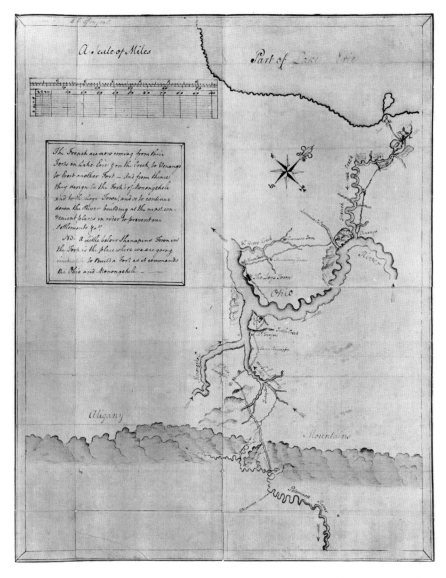

Washington's map of the Ohio, 1754, showing the route taken by Washington to meet the French. *Library of Congress, Geography and Map Division.*

on the frontier, pushing back the beginning of the Maryland Assembly's next session from February to the beginning of May.[63] While Dinwiddie and Virginia prepared for what appeared to be open conflict with the French, to the colonial government of Maryland, the showdown in the Ohio Valley was of no concern.

In early February 1754, the Ohio Valley was again thrust into the center of Maryland politics. The *Maryland Gazette* reported that a letter had been received from the governor of Virginia on February 5 that caused great concern to Sharpe.[64] In this letter, Governor Dinwiddie advised Sharpe that he was calling on him for assistance and that any force Sharpe could provide was to meet with a force of Virginians at a place called Will's Creek on the Potomac River.[65] In this letter, Dinwiddie also reported to Sharpe that the French had fortified themselves in the Ohio country. The information gathered from Dinwiddie's messenger pointed to the French and Native forces continuing to grow stronger than the 1,500 that was reported in the fall.[66] In response, Sharpe told Dinwiddie that he hoped the Maryland Assembly, now with information of increased French activity, would allow him to raise a force to support Great Britain's right to the Ohio but also "protect these colonies from the insolence of those that want to disturb our peace."[67] With increased urgency, Sharpe issued a proclamation calling for the Maryland Assembly to gather on Monday, February 25, 1754.[68]

On February 26, the members of the Maryland Assembly gathered in the statehouse to hear Governor Sharpe's opening speech of the new session. In his speech, Sharpe explained the reason for the "inconveniences" of calling on the assembly "at this early season….The welfare of this and the neigbouring colonies might suffer from any longer delay."[69] Sharpe continued, "Alarmed at the prospect of seeing our common enemy masters of all the country adjacent to the inhabited parts of these provinces, his Majesty's faithful subjects in Virginia, solicit our aid to defeat their ambitious enterprise, in the event of which…you will think this Province too much interested not to exert yourselves on this occasion."[70] To really put the delegates in a bind, Sharpe recalled the words of the delegates from the previous session. While they did not approve Sharpe's requests, the delegates affirmed that they would support their neighboring colonies should the need arise. Sharpe's intent was to put the delegates in a position from which they had to renounce their previous position and either continue to refuse to help against the French or give Sharpe whatever support he needed to help the Virginians. To further get the need across and increase the pressure, Sharpe provided letters from the colonial governor of New York, James Delancey, and Massachusetts governor William Shirley, discussing the same issue Sharpe was placing before Maryland's delegates.[71]

Another interesting piece of information that Sharpe inserted into his opening address was his receipt of a letter from the lords of trade in

London about a conference that was to be organized in Albany, New York, during the summer of 1754. This letter, dated September 18, 1853, advised each colonial governor that King George II had authorized presents to be given to the Six Nations (the Iroquois), with the Governor of New York acting as the facilitator of the meeting during which the gifts were to be presented.[72] This meeting was of great importance, because it was feared that the influence of the French would result in the powerful nations of the Iroquois clashing with British arms when conflict broke out. The trade commissioners felt that the colonies "whose interest and security is connected with and depends upon them" were critical and recommended sending commissioners to the conference.[73] The only requirements for the appointed commissioners were that they had to be "men of character, ability, integrity, and well acquainted with Indian affairs."[74] In the dense woodlands of the North American wilderness, the support of the Native tribes, with their experience in woodland fighting and their ability to navigate through the wilds, was imperative. In earlier colonial conflicts in North America, the support of the Native tribes played an important role in how those conflicts played out. By reporting this letter to the gathered assembly, Sharpe again put pressure on the assembly to take action to prepare for the brewing conflict.

After Sharpe's speech, the thirty-nine members of the lower house proceeded to work on Sharpe's request. The day after Sharpe's speech, Delegates Matthew Tilghman and Dr. Charles Carroll presented before the lower house an address to Governor Sharpe that focused on his request. The Committee of Laws, the committee that wrote and proposed laws within the lower house and to which Tilghman and Carroll were assigned, stated within the address that the members will, "with a just regards to his Majesty's interest…consider the several letters laid before us by your Excellency, and we hope the result will be such to meet your approbation."[75] Despite those encouraging words, just a day later, the delegates of the lower house quickly put to bed any consideration for funding to provide men or material aid to Virginia. When the issue was put forward for a vote, it was voted down, and the issue, for the time being, was dead in the assembly.[76] This vote by the Maryland delegates against proceeding to raise any type of aid to assist their fellow colonies appeared to flow with the long-held view of the lower house delegates. Previous assemblies continually and adamantly voiced support for their sister colonies with the pledge to provide assistance. However, when given the chance, their actions were the exact opposite. Despite their refusal to support a bill that would help Virginia, the delegates approved the appointment of commissioners to attend a conference with the Iroquois that was to take place later in the year in Albany, New York.[77]

Sharpe's personal response to the delegates' vote is not known; however, from the writings of Virginia's Robert Dinwiddie, we may be able to glimpse Sharpe's anger. In a letter written to Sharpe on March 3, 1754, Dinwiddie made references to a February 27 letter in which Sharpe appeared to question the motivations and judgment behind the decision made by the assembly. Dinwiddie advised Sharpe that he did not know "how any person [could] presume to assert that we were to raise no forces," despite the call by Dinwiddie for assistance clearly stating that was the intent.[78] He went on to sympathize with Sharpe and his dilemma, stating that he was sorry "[Your] Assembly are [backward] in the Supplies, as it is a [command] from his [Majesty]."[79] To provide more ammunition for Sharpe in forcing the issue with the delegates in Maryland, Dinwiddie advised him that he had raised a force and was pushing to construct a fort in the Ohio country to defend Great Britain's claim or repel "force by force."[80]

Heeding Dinwiddie's advice, Sharpe made another much sterner appeal to the delegates to reconsider their decision. In an address to the lower house on March 2, Sharpe explained to the delegates, despite a reported "backwardness" in Virginia's effort to raise a force against the French, that it should not affect or slow their deliberations. He advised them that he had "received certain information of a Bill having passed both Branches of the legislature of that province [Virginia]…whereby the sum of ten thousand pounds was granted…in that important enterprise."[81] After providing the delegates with the price Virginia's general assembly was determined to pay for the upcoming campaign against the French, Sharpe hoped to prod them into action to match Virginia's effort.

Sharpe's effort was for naught. On March 5, despite the delegates agreeing to raise funds to purchase gifts for the conference with the Iroquois, their stance on providing military assistance to Virginia did not change. The delegates agreed that the security of Maryland was associated with the safety of neighboring colonies, and if attacked, they should provide mutual assistance to each other. However, their agreement stopped there. Responding to Sharpe, the delegates wrote, "As it does not appear to us that any invasion or hostile attempt has been made against this, or any other of his Majesty's colonies, we do not think it necessary to make any provision for an armed force, which must inevitably load us with great expence [sic]."[82] If—and only if—the French were to invade or make some forceful movement against Maryland or other British colonies, the assembly would raise or supply any military force.

The delegates' actions caused Sharpe's anger to boil over. In response, he offered a letter describing the efforts that were being taken by Virginia to prepare for the brewing conflict, including an effort to request one thousand Cherokee and Catawba warriors from the Carolinas. In his writing, Sharpe was no longer able to hold his temper.

> *I cannot think the reason offered in…yesterday's address sufficient for… refusing any alliance with the Virginians…and if we duly consider the present posture of Affairs in Virginia and on the Ohio, I believe we shall not doubt our being sufficiently authorized…to engage in the intended expedition, and to give our troops instructions to act in concert with those… in the neighboring colony. For my own part, I can see the transactions of these people, against whom our aid is solicited in no other light than that of flagrant acts of hostility.…The summons sent them to retire and relinquish territories…you see were answered with a letter of Defiance, and by them… the greatest violences were commited on several of our fellow subjects. 'Twas this behavior…that obliged the Virginians to enter on measures, which… we cannot, without the charge of inhumanity render abortive.*[83]

Sharpe explained that Virginia needed assistance. He pleaded with the delegates to act. They needed to follow the Virginians, and his only tool was to invoke a sense of honor within the delegates "to maintain the faith and confidence our neighbors have in us, by the honor of the British Crown, and the safety of these provinces."[84] Despite Sharpe's insistence on helping Virginia, the lower house steadfastly held its belief that the letter from the Earl of Holderness only required them to act defensively. Since Virginia had not been attacked by the French, assistance from an armed force of Marylanders was not necessary.[85] With the delegates deeply rooted in their position, Sharpe gave up the fight but did not shy away from showing his disappointment: "I am most sensibly affected at your absolute refusal to make such provision as the…affairs seem to require…the issue of your deliberations on that affairs has left me no place for satisfaction."[86] Sharpe hoped that the planned expedition by Virginia was successful so the refusal by the lower house's delegates to send help would not cause issues later.

Against the backdrop of this debate over Maryland's involvement in Virginia's expedition to the Ohio county, something positive did come from the discussions. Legislation was passed through the assembly that provided

"500 pounds current money" for the purchase of gifts for the Six Nations of the Iroquois and to cover the expenses of two commissioners to be selected from a group of four delegates: George Plater, Benjamin Tasker, Daniel Dulaney and Matthew Tilghman.[87] These funds were made available as a loan from the colony, with the repayment being covered by the business licenses provided to hawkers, peddlers and petty chapmen or the penalties imposed on those merchants who illegally conducted business within the colony. Months would pass before any benefits from the meeting with the Iroquois were realized, and fortunately, the bill passed just in time. In early March, Sharpe prorogued, or dismissed, the assembly until May.

Despite Sharpe's efforts to get Maryland involved in the expedition west, Virginia went on alone, and events continued rolling toward a confrontation in the densely wooded forest of the western frontier. By late April, a small force of Virginians was at Will's Creek when reports were received of the expected arrival of the French at the confluence of the Alleghany and Monongahela Rivers, where they formed the Ohio River. Whoever controlled this important junction, commonly referred to as the Forks of the Ohio, controlled the vast interior of eastern North America. Previously, a small group of Virginians, under Captain William Trent, had constructed a blockhouse at the forks to stake Virginia's claim to the site and operate it as a trading post. The arrival of the French forced Trent's small band to evacuate, and the French began construction on what would become Fort Duquesne. Under the command of George Washington, the small force of Virginians at Will's Creek, joined by a force of South Carolinians, marched toward the Ohio Country to press the French out. By the end of May, Washington's force was encamped in a place called the Great Meadows when Native allies came into his camp with news of a small French force nearby that had ventured out of Fort Duquesne. On May 28, Washington, with his Virginians and Mingo allies, came across the French encampment, and in the early dawn, shots rang out. In the early morning confusion, both Virginian and French blood was spilled.[88] The murder of a French officer by a Mingo only added fuel to the growing fire.[89] Unknown to Washington, this fateful encounter sparked the war that changed the North American continent forever.

As Washington and his colonial force marched west, the Maryland Assembly was called into session during the first week of May 1754. In his opening speech, Sharpe again looked down on the delegates of the lower house for their unwillingness to support their fellow colonists. "I might set before you the example of the several provinces around us, to warm and incite you to...emulation of the laudable zeal they have shown for the common cause."[90] Reminding the delegates that their fellow colonies, especially Virginia, were using actions and not just words against the French, Sharpe showed the delegates their backward ways when it came to offering support. Before pleading with the delegates to provide the commissioners to the Albany conference the freedom to act in concert with their fellow colonial representatives, Sharpe took one more jab at the gathered members: "But from a persuasion that you will be actuated by more noble principles, than such as arise from the fear of censure…the enterprise which the Virginians have begun, and the neighboring governments unanimously engaged to prosecute, is undertaken from the preservation of our common safety, and that it's miscarriage [would result] in the most fatal consequences."[91] Sharpe's amicable nature and willingness to work with the delegates for the common good was now gone. The beginning of this session was quite different, and Sharpe was placing the need to do something front and center.

The words in Sharpe's speech appeared to work. On May 15, the delegates approved £3,000 to assist the Virginians.[92] This funding was included a bill titled "For His Majesty's Service." However, the original bill was returned from the governor's council, referred to as the upper house, with amendments. The differences between the bills were hashed out in a conference that began on May 24. The primary issue raised in the discussions was the lower house's interest in using funds normally sent to the proprietor to help pay for the appropriation.[93] The upper house's role in the Maryland legislative process, acting in conjunction with Governor Sharpe, was to act as the protector of the proprietor's rights in the colony. As a result, they rejected the lower house's wish to divert some of the proprietor's funds toward this supply bill and dismissed further objections from lower house. At the conclusion of the conference, Sharpe called for both sides to salvage at least a portion of the bill that dealt specifically with the conference in Albany. In a close vote, the delegates approved funding for "a present to the allied Indians."[94] All in all, when the session was closed at the end of May, inroads had been made toward getting Maryland involved in the coming conflict. The next session, scheduled for July, proved to be the point of no return, as news of the events involving Washington and his Virginians on the frontier began reaching Annapolis, Williamsburg and other colonial cities in the region.

In the Thursday, June 13, 1754 edition of the *Maryland Gazette*, an account was published of the battle that took place between Washington's Virginians and the French.[95] The account stated that Washington, after learning of the location of a French encampment from Native allies, led a party of forty men against the encampment. But the French "observed them before they came up and speedily put themselves in Order of Battle....When the two parties approached...the French...gave the first fire."[96] Taking advantage of the report that the French fired first, Sharpe called the assembly into session in mid-July 1754 and appealed to the delegates to finally follow through with the instructions for the Earl of Holderness's 1753 letter calling for the colonies to meet force with force if the French were to encroach on British possessions in North America.[97] Sharpe exclaimed that "the design of the French must not be evident to everyone," as they had invaded and violently attacked the Virginians.[98] Sharpe advised the delegates that he had already called out the militia to act if necessary to protect Maryland's frontier settlements, as they were likely to be "the first exposed to the inroads of the enemy."[99] It was Sharpe's hope that while the assembly hammered out a better way forward, the trained citizens of Maryland's county militias would hold the line against any French advances.

The delegates immediately went to work. Within two days of opening the session, a committee of the lower house presented a plan for raising nearly £6,000 toward fighting the French.[100] The next day, an act for His Majesty's service was sent to the upper house, and on July 24, it was passed.[101] In just a week, what had taken Sharpe months to get through the assembly was finally passed. Maryland was going to do something in the brewing war. With funds in hand and the assembly dismissed for the foreseeable future, Sharpe could finally breathe a sigh of relief and focus on what he had to do. However, a new and much larger task would soon fall at his feet.

Prior to the emergency session of the assembly, Sharpe was commissioned as the lieutenant colonel of the West Indies by King George II.[102] He was to be the man in charge of the military campaign to expel the French from Virginia and other parts of Great Britain's dominion in North America. Due to the nature of communication at the time, Sharpe did not receive his commission until October. In the meantime, Sharpe was in communication with Robert Dinwiddie. In late July, Dinwiddie wrote to Sharpe seeking advice on the construction of a fort by North Carolinian Colonel James Innes who now acted as commander in chief of the combined colonial force that was forming in Virginia.[103] The construction of this fort was paramount, as Dinwiddie feared that if there was a delay, the French would be reinforced.[104] Sharpe's response to Dinwiddie or whether any advice was offered is unknown. However, from the letters written to Frederick Calvert, Lord Baltimore, Sharpe was active in raising forces and funds to fight the French. In August, Sharpe wrote that during the Albany meeting that took place, a plan for a union between the colonies in "order to more easily defend his Majesty's American Dominions against the French or any other hostile forces" was made.[105] He also stated that he had ordered the raising of a company or two of men from Maryland to assist the Virginians in pushing back the French before winter began.

In October, Sharpe received his commission, placing him in command of the forces that were set to campaign against the French in North America, and he set about planning for the expected expedition. Sharpe wrote to British secretary of state Sir Thomas Robinson that he intended to "raise 700 men immediately who will...be able in conjunction with the three independent companies [British forces raised in the colonies] to carry the Fort, called Fort Duquesne...before a reinforcement can be sent the garrison.[106] It was a difficult task to complete. He wrote to the colonial governors of Pennsylvania, New Jersey, New York, Rhode Island, Connecticut and Pennsylvania, advising them of the new task he had been given, and he asked that they place before their respective assemblies the need to support Sharpe's effort by raising either troops or money.[107] Sharpe also set about inspecting the defenses on the colonial frontier, especially the fort that was under construction at Will's Creek. What he saw did not give him confidence in the success of his campaign. At the fort—and under Sharpe's command—were three independent companies who did not meet Sharpe's expectations, 120 "discontented, unruly, and mutinous" Virginians and the incomplete Maryland company that Sharpe had ordered to be raised.[108] Further observations showed Sharpe that those officers with commissions in the British army "would not deign to rank with those who served under his Governor's Commissions," marking a drastic divide within the forces, as colonial officers were viewed as inferior to their British counterparts.[109]

While Sharpe was acting in his capacity as commander in chief of all British and colonial forces in North America, he also had to continue his duties as Maryland's governor. Returning to Annapolis from his travels on the frontier in early December 1754, Sharpe found that the political side of his effort to raise troops and money was finding mixed results. Governors Robert Morris of Pennsylvania pledged to "act up to the Royal Commands as fully as the Assembly of this province will enable me to do," while Governor Jonathan Belcher of New Jersey told Sharpe that "for near twelve Months past, I have been urging...several Assemblies of this province in the most pungent manner to fall into their Duty, by giving their Aid, & Assistance in Defence [sic] of...these Provinces."[110] The New Jersey Assembly was disbanded by Belcher for "turning a deaf ear," and after a second assembly was formed, the assembly appropriated funds—but only after it received an

The commission of Horatio Sharpe as lieutenant colonel of the West Indies. *Collection of the Maryland State Archives.*

answer from a petition sent directly to the king.[111] Receiving these responses and remembering his previous experience with the Maryland Assembly, Sharpe nevertheless attempted to gain further funding from the Maryland Assembly to support his efforts as commander in chief, even with his time in that role coming to end with the arrival of Major General Edward Braddock and two regiments from the British army in early 1755.[112]

Sharpe called the Maryland Assembly into session on December 12, 1754. His opening address, like his previous addresses, laid out all the transgressions the French were perpetrating against Maryland and their fellow colonies, including the construction of "several forts on his majesty's lands, one especially at a small distance from this province."[113] Sharpe painted the French in such a light that it seemed inevitable that the French were looking to expand into Maryland and that they would use any means necessary to do so, including sending French-leaning Native allies to terrorize the frontier.[114] In what amounts to an act of desperation, Sharpe placed his royal commission as the commander of the combined colonial forces in North America before the delegates of the assembly in the hopes that it would push them to act.[115] His hopes were ultimately dashed, as

General Edward Braddock.
Library of Congress.

the delegates again refused to raise funds, largely due to the inactivity of a neighboring colony (likely Pennsylvania) and their belief that before additional funding was approved, those funds needed to, in the form of printed money, circulate in the colony.[116] Of course, this avenue for raising funds was not agreeable to the upper house of the assembly, and the debate was ended for the moment.

Despite the ongoing debate within the Maryland Assembly and its refusal to act, reports continued to filter in from all points about the movement of the French on the colonial frontier. Letters arrived from other colonial governors, particularly those in New England, reporting that their respective assemblies were working to provide the necessary funding to prepare for war. And the continued construction of the fort at Will's Creek provided a speck of progress in a long winter of disappointments for Sharpe. By the end of February, Sharpe relinquished his commission as commander in chief when General Braddock arrived in Virginia.[117]

Upon the arrival of General Braddock, the general requested a meeting with the governors of each colony. However, Sharpe was unable to attend, as the Maryland Assembly was again in session beginning in late February 1755. As he did before, Sharpe painted a picture of a French force "remaining masters of those lands to the west" and implored the delegates to "fall on the most prudent...measures to raise as large a sum as the circumstances...will allow."[118] Sharpe presented a letter from British secretary of state Sir Thomas Robinson that outlined the forces that were being sent to the colonies and provided what was essentially a manpower quota that the colonies needed to raise to help fight the French. Robinson, in the letter, also advised Sharpe that he must raise the supplies that were needed for the army that was being sent and convince the assembly that a large sum of money was required to be contributed to a general fund. This general fund would be used to supply and raise the necessary forces.[119] This large sum was mentioned in Sharpe's opening address, with him urging the assembly to pass the required funds as quickly as possible.

The response from the delegates to Sharpe's opening address was a jab at both the governor's council in the upper house and Sharpe himself. As

"Freemen of Maryland," the delegates reminded Sharpe that they were still willing and able to act as needed.[120] However, they reminded Sharpe that the assembly was a bicameral legislature: "We…make but one branch of the legislature of this Province and that without the concurrence of the rest… nothing effectual can be done."[121] They resolved to work on the issues at hand, but this was clearly a shot across the bow of Sharpe and the upper house. If Sharpe wanted what he requested, then he had to work with the delegates; otherwise, the legislative process would grind to a halt with nothing being accomplished.

In March, the delegates in the lower house sent a bill titled "An Act for Raising a Further Supply Towards His Majesty's Service" to the upper house for passage.[122] The centerpiece of this bill included the large sum of money Sharpe was requesting that totaled £10,000. The upper house refused to pass this bill for two reasons. First, the delegates wanted to issue over £4,000 in paper money. The upper house did not think this was the proper course of action, believing that by issuing this amount of funds via paper would cause the money that was already circulating in the colony to depreciate.[123] The second reason involved yet another licensing fee that the delegates relied on to fund the previous supply bills that had been negotiated. The funds generated by this fee were already stretched thin for previous bills, and the upper house questioned why they should continue pulling money from it.[124] In addition to these reasons, the upper house believed that the bill did not do enough to show that it would be useful in expelling the French from the western frontiers. A lengthy reply from the delegates of the lower house laid out the case for why the bill should be passed. Among the objections, they challenged the members of the upper house to stop blocking the bill:

> *We could on our parts if it were regular, or they were wanting, suggest many reasons in support of our Bill, but we are persuaded we have already given such answers to your objections against it as cannot fail of convincing you of the Propriety thereof, in its present form. And we hope our fervent honest zeal for his Majesty's service, and the Common Cause, which has repeatedly actuated us to vote such generous Aids towards tendering effectual his royal intentions, will be no longer suppressed by your Honors nonconcurrance [sic] with the bill, we so long since formed for that very desirable end; and one more send up to you, as clear testimony to all the world of the sincerity of our designs on this important occasion.*[125]

The delegates were tired of granting Sharpe his funding and then having those bills repeatedly rejected because the funding source was pulled away from the funds that were being sent to Frederick Calvert, Lord Baltimore and lord proprietor of Maryland.

The stalemate in the legislature persisted throughout the session, as each house challenged the other over what sources were to be used to fund Sharpe's requested supply bill. The disputes became so intense that the delegates of the lower house asked that Sharpe end the session. They wanted to raise funds to support the war effort for the common cause, but the stubbornness of the upper house made remaining in session pointless, as nothing could be accomplished.[126] Sharpe continued pressing the issue, asking the delegates to find another source for the funding that did not touch the funds sent to the lord proprietor. The delegates, increasingly frustrated, again asked Sharpe to adjourn the session. Sharpe relented, and the assembly was prorogued and ordered to gather again in July.

The assembly returned in late June and immediately got to work preparing the supply bill for a war that was quickly escalating. During the preceding months, General Braddock gathered an army, including a contingent of Marylanders, and marched west toward Fort Duquesne. As the session moved along, a supply bill of £5,000, current money, was being contemplated.[127] While the assembly continued its work, reports were arriving regularly in Annapolis of attacks on the Maryland frontier, as settlers were being slaughtered or captured by French-allied Natives.[128] Sharpe reported these attacks to the assembly, which quickly resolved to raise a company of eighty men and supply them for four months.[129] Despite this quick approval to raise a small force to defend the frontier, the larger supply bill still caused issues within the legislature and ultimately failed. Another bill that focused on just the defense of Maryland's frontiers also failed. Each bill was considered by the delegates of the lower house, but the members of the upper house refused to pass either, and funds that belonged to the proprietor were again used. The session was concluded on July 8, 1755. A day later, disaster struck near the Monongahela River, just miles from Fort Duquesne, as elements of Braddock's army slammed into a French and Native force that was marching from the fort. In the ensuing three-hour-long battle, Braddock's force was decimated and routed. Braddock himself was mortally wounded and died just days later.

Following its defeat, Braddock's army, after losing nearly half its strength, retreated to the safety of the coast. This retreat left the frontiers of Maryland, Pennsylvania and Virginia protected by militia units that were not prepared

DEFEAT OF GENERAL BRADDOCK—9th July, 1755.

The defeat of Braddock, July 9, 1755. *Library of Congress.*

for what was to come. In Maryland, the situation quickly devolved into chaos. As settlers on the frontier fled east, little was being done in the assembly. For nearly a year, the delegates of the lower house repeatedly tried to pass bills to prepare the colony for its defense. However, those bills were rejected due to their source, Frederick Calvert's, Lord Baltimore's, proprietary funds. As the days moved into the fall of 1755 and early 1756, the colonial government of Maryland had to work together to accomplish something. The question was: could they?

3

"WE FACE THE BASTIONS AND CURTAINS WITH STONE AND SHALL MOUNT ON EACH OF THE BASTIONS A SIX-POUNDER"

MARYLAND PREPARES A DEFENSE

Just over a week after the defeat of Braddock's army at the Battle of the Monongahela, reports of the disaster that had taken place just miles from Fort Duquesne began reaching Annapolis. In the July 17 edition of the *Maryland Gazette*, against the backdrop of the French movements that took place farther north in New England, the editor reported, "We have been filled with concern, and a melancholy diffused, on some reports...of General Braddock's army having met with a severe blow from the French and Indians."[130] Those reports were confirmed later in the July 24 edition of the *Gazette* with news of Braddock's army suffering under a "very heavy and quick fire, which made great Slaughter among our men, and put them in great confusion."[131] Elsewhere, British fortunes were no better, as French incursions into New England captured several British forts on the frontier, opening yet another invasion route into the British colonies.[132] The middle colonies, Maryland, Pennsylvania and Virginia, were now practically defenseless against incursions by the French and their Native allies. Something had to be done, and it had to be done quickly. The year 1756 would prove to be a watershed year that prepared the Maryland for the growing conflict.

With news of Braddock's defeat reaching Annapolis, Horatio Sharpe found himself in a difficult position. He had just dismissed the Maryland Assembly in early July 1755 and was on the march west toward Fort Cumberland at the head of a small force of Maryland militia that was supported by what little funding the assembly had appropriated. He had to decide whether he would call the assembly back into session to face the rising emergency in Maryland or wait for developments. He decided to take the latter approach.

One of the big issues facing Sharpe was the need to convince enough men to join him in the defense of the colony. He wrote in a July 1755 letter that "it grieves me to see near 20,000 men in this Province fit to bear arms," but the assembly's inability to grant his request for a militia law meant he had barely 100 men to defend the colony.[133] To his brother William, Sharpe wrote that he "despairs…persuading the Assembly to prepare" a militia law or passing any "proper measure for the security or real welfare of their country."[134] Despite this disadvantage, Sharpe, acting as commander in chief, seized the opportunity.

While traveling on the western fringes of the colony, Sharpe ordered the construction of several small forts that served as Maryland's frontier defense.[135] These forts offered isolated settlers on the frontier shelter and provided reassurance to those who were contemplating fleeing east toward safety. Sharpe ordered the garrisons stationed at these forts to constantly patrol the frontier to keep lines of communication open and said that "if Indian parties venture to make incursions…give the alarm & dispose themselves in such a manner as to cut off their retreat."[136] Despite Sharpe's best efforts and the efforts of the small garrisons at the forts ordered to be built by Sharpe, including Fort Tonoloway, and the garrison at Fort Cumberland on the far western fringe of the colony, settlers on the frontier continued to suffer. He reported to Governor Robert Morris of Pennsylvania that nearly one hundred civilians in the area had been killed or taken prisoner, that their homes had been destroyed and that daily war parties made an appearance in the vicinity of Fort Cumberland.[137] In Pennsylvania, one colonist described the situation on the frontier as refugees flooded into the small town of Carlisle:

> *We, to be sure, are in as bad Circumstances as any poor Christians were ever in, For the cries of the Widowers, Widows, fatherless and Motherless Children…are enough to Pierce the most hardest of hearts. Likewise it's a very Sorrowful specticle* [sic] *to see those that escape with their lives not a Mouthful to Eat or Bed to lie on, or cloths to cover their Nakedness, or keep them warm.*[138]

These refugees had lost everything except their lives. In the colonial capital at Annapolis, the general feeling was that the city was "in no more danger of…being attacked by Indians than London."[139] However, the specter of a French and Native attack in the vicinity was on the minds of colonists, with one writing that "so entire was their defenseless situation that even a small part of twenty or thirty Indians, by marching in the night and skulking in the day time, might come upon them unawares in the dead of night, burn their houses, and cut their throats, before they could put themselves in a posture of defense."[140]

Despite his best efforts, Sharpe could only do so much in his capacity as commander in chief. Writing to his brother John, Sharpe's frustrations began to show:

> *We lose an Inhabitant sometimes by parties of Indians that make Incursions on our Frontiers while the dispute subsists between the lower house & us concerning the Approriation of Ordinary Lycence [sic] fines puts it out of my Power to protect or provide for the Safety of the poor wretches whose distant situation exposes them to the barbarities of our savage enemy.*[141]

The fines mentioned were a part of the proprietors' funding. As the war escalated and the threat of incursions into Maryland by French-backed Native war parties increased, Sharpe needed more funding to expand his effort to defend the colony. His frustrations boiled over when he responded to a letter from William Shirley, the overall British commander in North America. Shirley had proposed a congress of the colonies, much like the one conducted at Albany in 1754. Sharpe appreciated the gesture, but he understood that he would be unable to impress on Maryland's assembly the importance of sending commissioners to attend this congress or allowing those representatives to make decisions in real time without having to await instructions from the assembly. However, as Sharpe lamented, "some disputes that subsist between the branches of the legislature have for the present put an entire [stop] to all business."[142] Sharpe got his opportunity to influence and prod the assembly into action when he called it back into session in early 1756.

After months of inactivity, Sharpe called the assembly into session once again on February 22, 1756. In the opening session, Sharpe laid out what was expected of the thirty-three members of the lower house, as the war on the frontier with the French was rapidly escalating. Sharpe began his speech by advising them that Maryland would be expected to make an effort to meet the expectations of Major General William Shirley, who was now coordinating the British effort in North America. To add weight to this expectation, the governor described the state of affairs on the frontier. The former Native allies of the British, the Shawnee and Delaware, had, "with impunity…laid great part of three provinces desolate" and "flushed with victory they bid us defiance."[143] To respond to this crisis, Sharpe proposed two legislative priorities for the assembly to act on. The first was an act to prevent military supplies or provisions from being exported from the colony for use by the enemy, and the second was another request to revive the 1704 militia law. In Sharpe's opinion, the then-current militia law in the colony was insufficient, as it did not "oblige the service of any one in defence [*sic*] of their Country," and the safety of the colony depended on a militia "being well armed, disciplined, and under proper regulations."[144] Of the two requests, the militia law was Sharpe's primary focus for the session.

Descriptions of attacks on the western frontier of the colony, primarily those in Frederick County, served as constant reminders to the delegates of what was at stake. Early in the session, one such article in the *Maryland Gazette* described the death of several settlers and the destruction of their homes, leading the author to write that the accounts from the frontier "are truly alarming. All the Slaughters, Scalping, Burnings, and every other barbarity and Mischief that the mongrel French, Indians…can Invent, are often perpetrated there, and approach us nigher and nigher."[145] The first and easiest bill to pass through the assembly was the act concerning the movement of military stores or provisions out of the colony for use by the French. The passage of this bill was of the utmost importance, as Maryland was home to a substantial Catholic population, and there was constant fear that those citizens would do anything to assist the French. Introduced from the upper house on February 28, the bill was quickly passed.[146] The law was actually a continuation of a previous law that had been passed in June 1755, but it was allowed to lapse. It forbade anyone in the colony from carrying aboard a ship "ammunition, warlike stores, or provisions or denomination whatsoever, except for the necessary use of such ship or vessel," unless authorized by a naval officer and after paying a bond valued at £1,000 sterling.[147] It also forbade the export of these supplies via land routes that led out of the colony. The penalty for violating this act was the forfeiture of any supplies that were being carried and required a financial penalty that was double the value of the forfeited supplies, with the payment sent to the treasury of the colony for use in "His Majesty's service."[148] This law was to remain until March 1757.[149]

With Sharpe's first priority completed, the real issue that would dominate this session of the assembly took hold. Sharpe's hopes to further prepare

One of the most feared fates on the frontier was to be scalped during a Native raid. *Library of Congress.*

Maryland for its defense required the assembly to pass further funding that provided for some kind of military force to defend the colony. Those deliberations began in earnest in early March 1756. As part of the opening debate, the lower house requested information from Governor Sharpe about what steps had been taken by other colonies in their efforts to force a treaty with the "southern Indians."[150] They also requested that Sharpe inquire about the possibility of either Virginia or New York sending to Maryland "a quantity of his majesty's arms and ammunition" to be used by the colony and to request clarification on the arms the colony had temporarily issued to the independent companies and if they had been returned.[151] These two requests appear to show that the assembly, unlike in previous sessions, was taking the conflict that was devastating Maryland's frontier seriously. Replying to their requests, Sharpe advised the delegates that he had not received any information about how other colonies were negotiating with the southern tribes, the Catawba and Cherokee. However, in the absence of the plans these colonies had, Sharpe urged the assembly to provide whatever was necessary to "secure those Indians to the British interest" and to also empower those commissioners negotiating on the colonies' behalf to have the ability to act in such a way as to "improve the good disposition of the Catawba and Cherokee nations towards us."[152]

Each day, the delegates of the lower house considered how they could raise the funds required to pay for Maryland's military obligations, and as the deliberations dragged on, the threat to Maryland's frontiers only grew. The defenseless situation on the frontier was highlighted in a petition that Governor Sharpe shared with the delegates on March 2. The petition came from the inhabitants of Frederick County, a well-established county that covered the entirety of western Maryland in the 1750s. Those living in Frederick County, especially those in the western parts of the county, were suffering greatly from the Native raids. In their petition, they "earnestly entreated" Sharpe to help them avoid the "miseries that their neighbors in Pennsylvania had experienced and were still suffering."[153] By sharing this petition, Sharpe increased the pressure on the lower house to grant the funding that was needed. Going back to 1753, Sharpe was constantly looking to get funding for the defense of the colony, and now, with pressure increasing on him to do something, he placed more pressure on the delegates of the lower house to also do something.

Within a day of receiving the petition, a series of resolutions were presented to the delegates for their consideration. Those resolutions included one calling for the construction of a fort and four block houses on the western frontier of the colony and two hundred men to be employed as a garrison at those places. And those men were to be drafted, if needed, from the militia companies in the colony.[154] Not only did these resolutions present a military solution for the defense of the colony, but they also offered a financial incentive to entice men to serve. The proposed bounty of twenty-two shillings and six pence was available to those who volunteered to enter the service.[155] With the particulars presented, the delegates resolved to raise £11,000 for the purpose of raising these troops and preparing the defenses, £10 to the citizens of the colony and Native allies who presented scalps taken from a French-allied Natives, not to exceed £1,000; £3,000 to "cultivate the friendship and engage the alliance" of the southern Natives (Cherokee and Catawba); £10,000 to be "applied towards an expedition to the westward"; and £15,000 to be provided for carrying out Shirley's plans in the northern colonies.[156] In total, the funding for the proposed resolutions totaled £40,000 sterling, a substantial amount (just over $9.2 million today) when compared to previous funding bills of this nature.[157]

It's interesting to note that the delegates were able to quickly determine the specifics of this funding bill. For years, they balked at the prospect of raising funds to prepare the colony for a possible war, despite Sharpe's incessant requests to fund such efforts. Each of those previous requests ended with the delegates willing to make a halfhearted effort to give the governor what he wanted, but the means by which those funds would be raised—taking them directly from the proprietor's revenue—was unacceptable. Now, with the inevitable conflict threatening Maryland, the delegates finally acted with urgency. After less than two weeks of deliberation, the amount of spending they proposed matched the efforts of the colonial assemblies in Virginia, Pennsylvania and elsewhere. Again, the only issue that could possibly arise was where the appropriated funds would be drawn from.

To provide emergency funding for ranging parties and payments for enemy scalps or prisoners that were presented, the ways and means committee of the lower house delivered a plan that would raise the £40,000 in new money being proposed by the delegates. Over a period of five years, the committee proposed that various duties and taxes that were already in place would go toward repaying the proposed amount, while new taxes would be issued to cover any shortfall that may occur. Examples of these funding sources included taxes on all alcoholic items that were either imported or produced in the colony, horses that were purchased or sold and the importation of slaves and an increased tax on landowners per one hundred acres of land sold, including an additional tax on Catholic landowners, and a tax on land warrants for lands that were to be surveyed that were one hundred acres or less, with additional tax charged for every ten acres over the first one hundred.[158] These old and newly added taxes were expected to raise £7,953 per year and total just under £38,000 after five years.[159] The unused funds from the previous supply bill in 1754 were to be used to cover the remaining amount. Over the coming days, the particulars of the bill were debated and changed as the delegates voted on the specifics of the bill.

Sharpe's reaction was hopeful. Writing to Virginia's governor Robert Dinwiddie, Sharpe noted that after sitting for only eleven days, the "lower house of Assembly…passed a vote granting 40,000 pounds for his Majestys [sic] Service & the better defence [sic] of our frontiers."[160] While the delegates continued working on the spending bill, Sharpe received a commission from Major General William Shirley, commander in chief of British forces in North America, to raise and take command of a force of four thousand men from the southern colonies (Maryland, Virginia, North Carolina, South Carolina and Georgia) that were to launch a campaign against Fort

Duquesne.[161] While the lower house moved quickly to pass the funding bill, Sharpe was not optimistic that the funds would be made available by not only the Maryland Assembly but the assemblies of the colonies from which he was to raise this sizable provincial army. Just days after his hopeful letter to Dinwiddie, Sharpe took a much different tone in a letter he wrote to Major General Shirley. He remarked, "The Assembly of this province [Maryland]… has now met a fortnight but have not yet come to any determination" on the requests Sharpe had laid before them. Despite receiving the commission to command this army, Sharpe was apprehensive of his ability to raise such an army, as "the warlike spirit that has spread itself thro the Eastern Colonies has not…yet reached these regions.[162] Continuing, Sharpe stated that "these Provinces appear quite inactive," as he did not know what to expect from Virginia and the Carolinas.[163] The governor admitted that the amount of £40,000 had been approved but that "from experience I find there is a wide difference between voting a sum of money & granting or raising it," and even with that amount of money, it "will go but a little way towards raising & transporting the number of men that is deemed the quota for this colony."[164]

Finally, on March 27, the formal bill, An Act for Granting a Supply of Forty Thousand Pounds for His Majesty's Service and Striking Thirty-Four Thousand and Fifteen Pounds Six Shillings Thereof in Bills of Credit, and Raising a Fund for Sinking the Same, was introduced to the lower house by Robert Lloyd, a delegate from Queen Anne's County.[165] Four days later, the delegates got their chance to vote, and the bill was passed by a 34–16 vote.[166] The delegates of the lower house passed a bill that taxed, in their minds, the populace fairly, as it continued taxes that had been established in a previous supply bill. What it also did was tax the lands of the proprietor and looked to use the proprietor's revenue sources as a means to help pay for it, especially since a new line of credit was being created. The use of the proprietor's revenue was a constant funding source that had been long sought after by the delegates when it came to funding bills in Maryland. However, each time they attempted to use that source, they were rebuffed by the governor's council. The passage of the bill in this form set up the inevitable conflict, with the required approval of Sharpe and the upper house becoming increasingly doubtful.

While the supply bill was working its way through the legislature, the war on the frontier was not waiting. As the assembly was in session, Sharpe constantly sent updates to the delegates, keeping them aware of the situation in an effort to get a bill through the lower house that would meet the approval of the upper house. One such update included reports that inhabitants in

Pennsylvania were fleeing westward, leaving Maryland's settlements along the Pennsylvania border open to attack, as the French and their Native allies were reportedly pushing east.[167] In early April, with various units of Maryland Rangers set to return home, Sharpe shared information that a Native war party had "done some mischief on the frontiers, near Mill's Fort," in an effort to gain more funding to support those Marylanders.[168] Emergency funding was provided for the rangers. A report in the *Maryland Gazette* added further urgency to get the bill passed. Arriving from Conococheague, located near the foot of North Mountain, a large group of Marylanders, including thirty children, settled near Baltimore "to avoid the fury of the Enemy." The group had been surprised by a Native attack, resulting in the destruction of their homes and the loss of their livestock.[169] With the destruction on the frontier creeping eastward, the lower house of the assembly sent the £40,000 supply bill to the upper house for approval.

After examining the bill, the upper house, or governor's council, raised several objections. Their first was that the bill gave Sharpe the ability to decide where the colony's defenses are placed. In the lower house's bill, any forts or block houses constructed were to be built on the eastern side of North Mountain (today's Fairview Mountain near Clear Spring, Maryland).[170] The council also wished for the lower house to appoint a commissary to oversee the procurement and distribution of supplies and to accurately maintain muster rolls of the men who enlisted.[171] They wished for Sharpe to have the ability to keep men in the field past the December 25 deadline established by the delegates if the governor believed they were needed "for the security of the Province or the more effectual annoyance of the enemy."[172] Finally, the council believed that upon the discharge of the militia, which was currently acting as the primary force in Maryland's defense, an equal number of men should be selected from various county militias to ensure that a substantial amount of men were in the field at any given time. The members of the upper house also presented what the sizes of the companies should be, what military ranks should be used and the pay for those ranks.

After stating its objections, the council presented items within the bill that it rejected outright. Those rejections focused largely on the lower house's effort to raise funds via the specific taxes and duties. The council argued it was the "right of the government" to appoint tax collectors and that to place a tax on wine and other spirits already in private hands was an "unprecedented, unheard of tax and of dangerous tendency under a British Constitution." It also said that a tax on the importation of horses was unjust, as there was already a law in place prohibiting their sale within Maryland.[173]

Frederick Calvert, the sixth Lord Baltimore and Lord Proprietor of Maryland. *Courtesy Enoch Pratt Free Library, Maryland's State Library Resource Center.*

The council also specifically mentioned that it could not consent to the delegates appropriating funds received from quit rents that went directly to the proprietor Frederick Calvert without the permission of the proprietor.[174] Quit rents were remnants of the feudal system that allowed a single person— in this case, Frederick Calvert—to charge a small annual fee to a person who received a land grant.[175] In addition to rejecting the previously mentioned taxes and fees, the council also rejected the new land tax that the delegates were seeking—the first of its kind, according to historian J. William Black.[176] This specific tax affected not only those who had already received land grants from the proprietor but also the proprietor himself, as it required him to produce a survey of lands to provide an accurate account of his lands that remained unoccupied. With these and the other requested changes, the council returned to bill to the lower house delegates.

After receiving the upper house's objections, it took one day for the delegates to respond. Writing in response, the delegates stated they "are to [*sic*] deeply sensible of the distresses of our frontier-inhabitants, and that dangers which threaten his Majesty's American Dominions," but despite the increasing debt from remaining in session, they could not agree with the changes.[177] Answering what they considered an "unparliamentary message," the delegates were concerned that the objections would result in over £34,000 being taken out of the bill. The issue must have been pressed, because they presented the funding bill as required, since it was within their "rights and privileges" to set how and where appropriations came from.[178] In response, the upper house blamed the delegates for unnecessarily extending the session, and despite being called into session specifically for the purpose of passing a funding bill, the delegates wasted nearly two months before sending the bill to the council.[179] With the back and forth between the two houses, the passage of this much-needed bill was turning into a nightmare.

The stalemate over the supply bill was increasing Governor Sharpe's frustration. In a letter to Major General William Shirley, Sharpe apologized and stated that "the measures taken by the Assembly of this province...to grant any supplies obliges me to acquaint your Excellency that I have...very little hopes of seeing such a number of men raised by them this summer."[180] Time was of the essence, and the failure of the assembly to act did not bode well for the 1756 campaign season. The French and their Native allies were attacking the frontier with impunity, despite Sharpe's best efforts to get men into the field. It just wasn't enough, as Sharpe stated, "Our westernmost settlements have been for some time cut off & the country laid waste for 60 miles on this side of [Fort Cumberland]," and the inhabitants fled at the slightest hint of danger.[181] In describing the hopelessness of the situation, Sharpe was surrendering any hope he had in the legislature telling Shirley that he "must give over all thoughts of getting any troops from this Province" and pleaded with the general to order him to march on Fort Duquesne with the troops he had.[182]

With Sharpe frustrated over the lack of progress in the legislature, the two houses of the assembly continued their back-and-forth arguments, charging each other with wasting time. In a letter to the upper house in mid-April, the delegates acknowledged that it did take a "good deal of time" to get their bill together, but "perhaps a week spent in an imperfect consideration may not be thought inadequate to near seven [weeks] in drawing and framing it."[183] The continued back and forth finally ended with the upper house's outright rejection of the supply bill as it stood. Ending the debate, the members of the upper house reprimanded the delegates for continuing what they perceived to be an injustice, stating they did not have time or see the need to "enter into controversies…which can produce no good effect."[184] In one final point, the upper house, despite whether its objections were removed or not, believed its conduct justified and made clear to "all impartial and indifferent persons how fruitlessly we have done our efforts for the relief of the distressed people on the Western frontiers."[185] If the blame for the failure of the bill fell on anyone, it fell squarely on the lower house.

Forced to start over, Sharpe began asking the assembly for funds. When the funds that supported the few forces Sharpe managed to get into the field were used up, the governor used his own personal funds to continue supporting them. Pleading with the lower house, Sharpe wrote, " I hope you will not hesitate to make some farther provision for the support of those parties and my reimbursement."[186] The delegates responded that a bill was in the works that was "well calculated to protect our frontier, which if passed into law, will render the ranging parties…of no use."[187] This new bill was similar to the previous bill, meaning that upon its arrival in the upper house, the council rejected it in its current form. However, instead of sending it back to the delegates to be reworked, the members of the upper house, in an effort to "demonstrate our strong inclination to do everything in our power for…the defense and preservation of the Western frontiers," proposed a conference to "produce the desirable end."[188] Despite this possible step in the right direction, Sharpe remained frustrated, especially with the delegates who believed it may be necessary for him to end this session of the assembly.[189] To Sharpe, time was running short, and something had to be done.

The conference between the two houses was set to take place in early May 1756. The attendees included Phillip Thomas and Benjamin Tasker representing the upper house and Delegates Phillip Hammond, Edward Tilghman, William Murdock, Matthew Tilghman and "Mr. Carroll" representing the lower house.[190] Beginning on May 6, this small group worked to solve the differences between the two houses. For the next six days, the two sides settled their differences, and the bill, with a few exceptions, survived intact. The fact that this conference took place at all boosted Sharpe's hope. Writing to Governor Dinwiddie in Virginia, Sharpe said, "Our Assembly is still sitting, some gents [sic] from each house have been more than a week conferring...on the supply bill. I believe there will be one passed," but it was possible that whatever made it through the assembly would still not be enough.[191]

Sharpe's wait was short lived. On May 12, the delegates of the lower house approved the amended bill, sending it to the upper house for a final approval.[192] With the bill's passage, the delegates hoped the upper house members would pass the bill into law, allowing for a repayment to Sharpe for his personal contribution to the ranging parties on the frontier, which, by then, were unnecessary, with the bill allowing for the creation of a more permanent force.[193] In the upper house, the bill was brought to the attention of Governor Sharpe himself, who offered a few final alterations that were rejected but still resulted in the final passage of the bill on May 14, 1756.[194] With the bill's passage, Sharpe finally had the funds he needed. The bill's passage became official on May 22, when it was entered into law, and after years of debate, stalemate and needless delay, Maryland was ready to go to war. Sharpe wasted little time in putting the funds to use.

Within a month, Sharpe was leading a delegation of soldiers, carpenters, stonemasons and other craftsman to a small plot of soil in western Maryland, where he decided to construct what became the backbone of the colony's defense. Sitting on a slight rise about a mile from the Potomac River, the massive stone walls of Fort Frederick, named for proprietor Frederick Calvert, began to rise. In August, after returning to Annapolis, Sharpe wrote to Robert Dinwiddie that the fort under construction was being completed by troops he left there and that "we face the bastions & curtains with stone & shall mount on each of the bastions a six pounder."[195] By the end of the year, the construction of the fort was far enough along that there were four cannons mounted in each of its bastions, and a garrison of some two hundred men supported by an additional two hundred militiamen who patrolled the area to the east of the fort.[196] Sharpe was also hopeful that now

An artist's depiction of Fort Frederick. *Historic American Buildings Survey, Library of Congress.*

that this fort was under construction, the assembly would continue acting in harmony with Sharpe's efforts and would not "blame me for constructing the fort of stone [and] earth instead of wood," therefore making the expense of the fort's construction much greater.[197]

The year 1756 proved to be a turning point in Maryland's involvement in the war. After weeks of back-and-forth debate, the Maryland Assembly granted Sharpe his wish for funding. But Sharpe had to surrender some of the proprietor's funds—funds he was sworn to protect—to do so. With Maryland raising troops and providing materials for the war, the next two years would test the colony. Its resolve would be challenged, and the debate over its involvement in the war would continue. But for the moment, Maryland was completely committed.

4

"THE CIRCUMSTANCES OF OUR CONSTITUENTS"

MARYLAND'S EFFORT STALLS

The passage of the 1756 funding bill was a significant progression in Maryland's participation in the French and Indian War. As historian Aubrey C. Land noted, the lower house had successfully managed to increase its power within the political structure of the colony. First, it was able to dictate how the funds were to be spent and established a commission that would guide the defense of the colony and manage the relations with allied Native tribes.[198] It was also, in a rather significant way, able to divert funds from the proprietor to pay for the bill.[199] While the delegates gained power, Sharpe was also able to get what he had long desired. Acting as both the political and military leader of the colony, Sharpe needed the assembly to appropriate funding to properly defend the colony. Unfortunately, Sharpe and those he delegated to properly spent the £40,000 and quickly burned through the funds. The largest draw on the funds was the construction of Sharpe's vision for Maryland's defense, the stone-walled Fort Frederick, and the raising, outfitting and supplying of several companies of Maryland soldiers. With Maryland committed to the war in the short term, 1757 and 1758 would test whether that commitment would endure with legislative infighting taking place against a backdrop of ever-increasing violence on the frontier.

After a brief session in later 1756 that saw the assembly and Sharpe haggling over the needed funds for a royal regiment of Americans, colonists enlisted under the auspices of the king, the colony appeared to be in position to defend itself quite well. Sharpe had, at times, personally overseen the construction of Fort Frederick. Enlistments in the Maryland infantry companies were going well, and militiamen were serving alongside the provincial troops on the frontier as needed. New leadership had arrived in North America to direct these affairs, and 1757 was to be yet another year in which British leadership, now under the command of John Campbell, the earl of Loudoun, pressed colonial governors and legislatures to fund and prepare for another campaign season.[200] Writing to his brother Gregory, Governor Sharpe felt that the effort was a fruitless cause: "I presume he will desire us to press our respective Assemblies," referencing a continued need for supplies for an offensive campaign in the summer.[201] Sharpe continued, "I hope the execution of his [Lordship's] plan is not to depend on the resolutions of any American Assemblies.…Few of our people seem to be sufficiently sensible of all the dangers that threaten them & few disposed to contribute generously.…They have talked in Virginia & in this province more particularly of disbanding [the colonial forces that were gathered].[202] Sharpe's optimism that not only the Maryland Assembly but other assemblies as well would go along with Loudoun's plans was clearly not very high. Ever the dutiful servant, however, Sharpe would make any effort he could to benefit the cause.

While Sharpe was originally planning to call the assembly into session in late January 1757, an outbreak of smallpox in Annapolis forced him to continually push back the opening session.[203] The smallpox outbreak was not Sharpe's only problem. Seven companies of the royal American regiment were quartered in Annapolis for the winter. Maryland's recruitment for the regiment was suffering, despite the offer of a bounty, and recruits were deserting, with dozens waiting for their punishments to be carried out. Another reason for concern was that Maryland's primary defensive structure, Fort Frederick, was undermanned in Sharpe's eyes. The fort's garrison was expected to number 300 but "scarcely amounts to 250 men," and Sharpe believed "the officers will find it impossible to raise the number allowed for the immediate defence [sic] of this province."[204] The only good news was that no major disruptions had taken place on the frontier, and there was a sense that the frontier was becoming relatively safe.[205]

With all of these issues, Sharpe's pressing need to get the assembly into session to prepare the funding needs for the year forced him to move the session's location. On April 8, 1757, the newest session of the assembly opened in Baltimore, thirty miles away, to avoid a persistent smallpox outbreak in Annapolis.[206] While funding for the war was the focus of the session, the requests were not coming from Sharpe but from the commander in chief of the British war effort in North America, the earl of Loudoun, John Campbell. The funding requested included a troop quota that Maryland was to provide to the planned summer campaign against the French. Sharpe was hopeful that the delegates would act quickly and "give such dispatch to the business on which we are assembled, as the present posture of affairs, and the advanced season, require."[207]

Delivering the usual remarks at the opening of the session, Sharpe shared Lord Loudon's plans for the coming campaign. Loudoun's plans called for each colonial governor, including Governor Sharpe, to impress on their respective assemblies certain requirements. The delegates reviewing the documents read requirements that included an agreement by the governors that wagons for royal troops were to be provided at a reasonable price, and, either in a permanent or temporary fashion, proper quarters for those royal troops were to be stationed in the colonies. As a participant in this meeting, Sharpe had agreed to Loudoun's requirements. The agreement concerning the quartering of the king's soldiers was a particular concern of the delegates. The delegates believed that Sharpe did not have the power to make that agreement. In their minds, there were no laws of England or Maryland that allowed for the quartering of troops at any time, and if there were, the delegates requested that Sharpe inform them of "the custom by which you are vested with such authority." In reply, Sharpe was unsure of the law or regulation that provided him the authority to make the agreement. However, Sharpe told the delegates that other governors who participated in the meeting were told directly by the king to "use their utmost diligence and authority in procuring an exact observance" of Loudoun's orders.[208] In the course of his reply, Sharpe also put before the delegates a law that would allow royal troops to be housed in Maryland. Sharpe believed he had the authority to unilaterally allow this to take place, but to alleviate any possible conflict, the governor wished for the delegates to pass legislation to settle the quartering issue.[209] Sharpe's insistence that the delegates pass legislation became an ongoing theme in the politics of colonial Maryland. Sharpe's authority to do what was needed to wage war was limited. He needed help from the delegates of the lower house.

The primary purpose of this session was to pass another bill providing further troops and funding to meet the quota set by the Earl of Loudoun. While admonishing Sharpe about troop quartering, the delegates were busily working toward this goal. On April 16, a resolution was passed that allowed additional manpower to be raised, with a total number, including those already in service, not exceeding five hundred men.[210] While working on this resolution, the delegates also reported that a substantial amount, over £7,000 sterling, remained from the 1756 supply bill. To support the new enlistments, the delegates reappropriated a portion of these funds to outfit and maintain the Maryland forces that worked with British forces, while a sufficient number remained behind at Fort Frederick to defend Maryland's frontier.[211] Despite the passage of the resolution, Sharpe wrote to Loudoun, believing the assembly would not move quickly to meet his request. "They have been prevailed on to vote 500 men for the Defence of this Province," Sharpe wrote, "but, as they are exceedingly tedious in doing business, I am afraid 'twill be some time before I shall be empowered by an Act of Assembly to order the additional companies to be raised."[212] Sharpe shared a similar sentiment with Colonel John Stanwix, Sixtieth Regiment of Foot and British commander of the Southern District in the colonies."[213]

A few days later, the lower house sent the 1757 funding bill to the councilmen of the upper house for consideration. The upper house took the bill up on April 23 and, after making minor changes, approved the bill for passage, and returned it to the delegates for them to complete the amendments.[214] The lower house agreed to most of the amendments due to the nature of the request and the need to move quickly. However, there were amendments that "the circumstances of our constituents" did not allow them to approve.[215] Among the amendments at issue, the delegates believed that five hundred men were a sufficient force to defend the colony and that they met the manpower quota set by Lord Loudoun. Sufficient funds had been provided to complete Fort Frederick, making further funding unnecessary, and of the five hundred men in the Maryland Forces, a quantity were to remain at Fort Frederick to protect the supplies gathered at the fort.[216] Other disagreements dealt with the embezzlement of public funds, the need for proper muster rolls to be maintained, including returning men on furlough or missing to the rolls, and the delegates believed that the process that assisted those who were maimed or rendered incapable of providing for themselves or their family should remain unchanged.[217] The primary disagreement, however, focused on the upper house's suggestion that Governor Sharpe, or the person who was in command at the time, had the power to order all of Maryland's forces out of the colony, leaving the Maryland militia to defend the frontier. The lower house believed that this measure only increased the amount of funding the colony would spend, because in the absence of Maryland's provincial regulars, the militia defending the frontier would have to be put into the pay of the colony.[218]

The lower house again sent the bill to the upper house. The members agreed to forgo further debate on most of the amendments the delegates raised issue with in an effort to quickly get the bill passed. However, there were still a few amendments that they believed they could not consent to, including Sharpe's power to order the Maryland's forces away from the colony to serve elsewhere, the protection of the military stores at Fort Frederick, the use of proper muster rolls and a penalty instituted on officers falsifying their rolls.[219] With those objections, the bill was again returned to the lower house for approval. The issue here continued to be the lower house's attempt to gain a say in how the Maryland forces were being used, despite Sharpe being the commander in chief of the colony. Since Sharpe and the upper house were appointed by the proprietor, the power within the colony rested with the upper house. However, it needed the lower house to create bills in relation to important topics. Since Sharpe's arrival in 1753 and the outbreak of hostilities in 1754, the lower house had been attempting to seize a bit more power for itself. In this bill, that power included the ability to have a say in where and how the Maryland forces were being used.

Following yet another round of negotiations, the lower house added amendments it approved of and sent the bill back to the upper house, which took it into consideration on May 2. Again, the upper house made its own changes to the bill. These changes included mentioning funding dedicated to pursuing treaties with the "southern Indians," how funds were dedicated to payment for specific positions and the specific wording of certain phrases in the document.[220] The members of the council also wished for the lower house to establish, in law, that Horatio Sharpe was the governor and commander in chief of the colony and that he, or a person serving in the position, was the sole decision-maker when it came to how the Maryland forces were to be used.[221] They also focused on how a certain portion of the funds for the support of the Maryland forces was to be used. To protect against embezzlement, the councilmembers suggested that recruiters for the respective companies had to provide receipts that showed the enlistment bounty had been offered and given to the recruit.[222] Muster rolls remained a point of contention, as the timing of the completion of the rolls—monthly while stationed in Maryland and bimonthly outside the colony—would affect soldiers' pay. The musters had to be completed before payment was issued.[223] Other instructions regarding soldiers' pay while on furlough, court martials and penalties for falsifying muster rolls were added, and the approved amendments were sent back to the lower house.

The lower house, just as it had in previous sessions, continued to have issues with the amendments made by the upper house. The constant back and forth between the houses caused the delegates to accuse the upper house of being "irregular and unparliamentary" due to the council's repeated and consistent attempts to make changes to funding bills.[224] To members of the lower house, the legislative process for any funding bills—or those "for grants of aids and supplies"—began with them, and those bills could not be changed by the upper house.[225] If the upper house was able to continue making alterations to approved bills to the extent that those changes resulted in a new bill, this caused the "manifest destruction of one of the most valuable privileges" of the lower house.[226] Begrudgingly, the delegates introduced a new bill to include the changes made by the upper house, and it resulted in the passage of the bill through the assembly.[227]

Despite the approval of the assembly, when the bill reached Governor Sharpe's desk, the governor questioned the delegates' definition of the word *frontier* when it came to Maryland's western lands. This issue arose from a passage in the bill that stated that at any time, a portion of the five hundred men raised by the colony "shall be employed in ranging about the frontier," while the remainder are to be left at Fort Frederick.[228] Sharpe's interest in this phrasing was largely due to an order issued to one of Maryland's colonial officers, John Dagworthy, who had taken a detachment of Marylanders to Fort Cumberland to garrison that place in the absence of the Virginians who were being sent elsewhere.[229] Irritated and refusing to define the boundary of Maryland's frontier, Sharpe, sent a message to the delegates, stating that by refusing to define a boundary, the paymasters "will not think themselves at liberty to issue any pay or subsistence to the men…posted at Fort Cumberland."[230] To keep paying the garrison, it's possible that Sharpe would be forced to abandon the fort and the stockpile of military supplies gathered there. This was a topic that was already considered and rejected by the delegates, as they felt it unreasonable to use Marylanders to garrison the isolated western fort.[231] Sharpe allowed the issue to go unresolved and dismissed the assembly.

Despite the back-and-forth nature of the politics in Annapolis that ended with the passage of two laws in 1756 and 1757 that supported Maryland's efforts in the war, one of the objectives specifically called for in the laws came to fruition. In the spring of 1757, a Cherokee war party made its way north from the Cherokee towns in what is today western South Carolina and eastern Tennessee. Invited by Virginia to "take up the hatchet" against the Shawnee and other French-allied Native tribes, the Cherokee, led by Wahachy of Keeowee, traveled from Winchester, Virginia, and arrived at Fort Frederick in late April.[232] From Fort Frederick, Wahachy intended to lead his warriors into the frontiers of Virginia, Pennsylvania and Maryland to fight alongside the provincials, with the intent to stay "as long as amongst our Brothers as there is use of us."[233] Taking the opportunity to seek a treaty with the Cherokee, Sharpe sent in late May a delegation, John Rideout and Daniel Wolstenholme, to the fort with a gift of one hundred pounds and other gifts to solidify the friendship and alliance between Maryland and the Cherokee.[234] The resulting treaty affirmed the Cherokee's commitment to fight the French and their Native allies and Maryland's commitment to supply the Cherokee with whatever they may need. In the course of the conference, Rideout and Wolstenholme served as representatives of Governor Sharpe, who hoped the alliance would continue as "long as the Sun and Moon shall endure" and that the Cherokee would "let our men go out to war with you. Look on them as your Brethren. Teach them to fight after your manner."[235] In one of their first acts together, Lieutenant Evan Shelby of Captain Alexander Beall's company of Marylanders joined a party of sixty-two Cherokee warriors who set out from Fort Frederick to patrol the countryside. In mid-May, the group began following the tracks of an enemy war party, surprising them on Allegany Mountain in the early morning hours of May 13 and killing four and capturing two.[236] With this success, over the course of the ensuing months, the Maryland forces would spend valuable time with their Cherokee allies, learning their ways of war.

Over the course of nearly two years, from 1755 to 1756, Native raids had decimated the colonial frontier, and the Marquis de Vaudreuil, the governor general of New France, wrote that French-coordinated Native raids had decimated the frontiers of Pennsylvania, Virginia and Maryland and that "the sufferings throughout the English colonies could not be greater."[237] Even with the new Cherokee alliance, the raids by the French-allied Delaware and Shawnee tribes continued into 1757. In June, waggoners were reported to have been killed about a mile Fort Frederick.[238] These attacks stretched into more settled areas of Maryland, including two attacks in July and August near the town of Frederick that resulted in the deaths of two colonists, the imprisonment of another and the destruction of a home, leaving a family of ten homeless.[239] However, with provincial forces mobilized and reinforced with Cherokee warriors, the war on the frontier began to turn. With the help of their Cherokee allies, provincial forces began to fight back. In June,

Brother Wahachey of Kaway & Brethren of the Cherokee Nation   15

  I have Received the Message You Sent by Mr. Rofs to advise me of Your Being Come to Fort Frederick. I Rejoice at Your Arrival and I bid You Welcome by this String of White Wampum Brethren I have heard of Your Fame & Your good Intentions towards us from Your Brother of Virginia & have for a long time had a great desire to see You, but it happens now You are Come; I am Unable to Meet You, this I Am Sorry for but I hope You will Excuse me since, I have Sent Mr. Walshahstone & Mr. Ridoult to Communicate my Sentiments to You, I have Appointed them, because I know that they have a particular Regard for You, & Because I am Confident they will Deliver my Words Faithfully; they will in my Name and in Behalf of the People of Maryland make a League with You which I hope will Last as long as the Sun and Moon shall Endure to Confirm it I present You this Belt of Wampum ———

Brethren
  When Mr. Rofs was to me I gave him Orders to Supply You with Such provisions as You should Stand in Need of, as a farther Mark of my Friendship towards You, I now Send You a present, Was it in my Power, I would Send You a larger, but as it is not, I hope You will not Consider the Value of the present, so much as the Inclination of him that gives it ———

Brethren
  Now we have made a League of Friendship and are known To Each Other, I will speak to You more freely on the purpose for Which You are Come; You say that Your good Brother the Governor of Virginia, has Signified to You that our Father King George Desires you will join the English, and Declare War against the French and their Indians, who without any Just Cause or provocation have fallen upon our people and Scattered their Bones over ye Country You also tell me that upon our Fathers Pleasure being made known to You, You have taken up ye Hatchet against our Enemies, and that You will hold it fast till You have used it against the French & the Indians in their Alliance; I am well pleased that You have already Taken such a Resolution, I hope You will soon make our Enemies ———

532

Horatio Sharpe to the Cherokee Natives. *George Washington Papers, Library of Congress.*

a Virginian and a group of about one dozen Cherokee warriors returned to Fort Cumberland with news that they had attacked a party of Frenchmen thirty-five miles from Fort Duquesne.[240] Later in the year, Lieutenant James Riley presented a captured French soldier to the Maryland Assembly following a skirmish near Fort Cumberland.[241] The defense of the frontier was finally turning around, despite continued conflict between Sharpe and the assembly.

In late September 1757, Sharpe called a newly elected assembly back into session to focus on the needs for the colony's defense, including housing for two regiments of British army regulars in Maryland. According to Sharpe, there was an expectation that the lower house would pass a bill to sufficiently accommodate two British regiments in the colony.[242] The earl of Loudoun could order regiments to Maryland, but it was the view of the delegates that a large force, in this case, well over one thousand officers and men, could not be sheltered in Maryland, as there were "few towns that have more than one or two inns or public houses in them."[243] Instead, in a rare act of agreement, both the lower house and Sharpe agreed that the colony would be able to handle a single regiment, with Sharpe raising those concerns with Loudoun.[244]

The first fight of the session began when Sharpe advised the delegates that he had ordered two companies of militia to patrol the frontiers due to an increased threat and reports of raids in Virginia.[245] The militia was called on without the advice of the delegates, due to the garrison at Fort Frederick being "too weak and sickly" to properly protect the frontier inhabitants. The delegate's reaction was one of concern. It was the view of the delegates that despite funding what they considered to be a sufficient force to protect the frontier, they could not approve Sharpe's order to call out the militia, even if Sharpe only intended to replace the militia companies already serving. To the delegates, ordering out the militia and putting them into the pay of the colony before relying on the force already funded made little sense.[246]

In raising issue with the use of the militia, the delegates were also called on to pass another supply bill to keep Maryland forces in the field. On top of this request, an additional request was received from Captain John Dagworthy, who was commanding the Maryland garrison at Fort Cumberland. In a letter that was written to Sharpe and subsequently shared with the delegates, Dagworthy reported that the garrison was running low on provisions.[247] In an attempt to supply the garrison, Sharpe requested that the delegates fund these Marylanders, as funds from the previous supply bills had been expended.[248] The request surprised the delegates of the lower house. The

Cunne Shote, a Cherokee chief, showing an example of trade goods given by Maryland. *From the New York Public Library.*

fact that Marylanders were garrisoning Fort Cumberland explicitly went against the previous supply bills that stated exactly where Maryland's forces were to be.[249] In criticizing Sharpe, the lower house believed that any consequences resulting from this garrison not being where they should be fell directly at the feet of the person who was responsible for their position, the earl of Loudoun, John Campbell. Sharpe reprimanded the delegates for this criticism, stating that Campbell was well within his rights to order the Marylanders there, since he held a royal commission as commander in chief and could shift troops around as he saw fit.[250] Sharpe implored the delegates to supply the garrison, as the lower house "will alone be answerable to the consequences" for not supporting the garrison, including the likely loss of valuable artillery and military supplies to the enemy.[251]

In addition to this squabble over supplying the garrison at Fort Cumberland, the goal of the session was to pass yet another supply bill to support those forces Maryland already had in the field and to prepare for quartering regular British troops over the winter. Early in the session, the delegates appointed two committees to estimate the cost of maintaining troops in the field and to quarter at least one thousand regular British troops in the colony. The results of the committee's work were presented on October 20, with the combined estimates totaling roughly £15,000 sterling. Despite having this information, the delegates delayed for over a month before acting.

Fort Cumberland. *From* History of Cumberland (Maryland), *by William Lowdermilk.*

Publicly, Sharpe continued to impress on the delegates that they must continue funding the war effort. Privately, it was an entirely different matter, as he began questioning whether the assembly wanted to keep troops in the field. In a letter to Governor Dinwiddie of Virginia, Sharpe stated that the assembly was considering the disbandment of Maryland's troops and letting the frontier settlements defend themselves.[252] Before he even convened the assembly, Sharpe knew that additional funding was needed and that it was likely the delegates would again pursue the needed funding from the proprietor's income and landholdings, an action that Sharpe could not condone for a second time.[253] With the days quickly ticking away, Sharpe believed that the delegates were simply looking to run out the clock on the new supply bill and force the governor to sharply rebuke the members. In a message to the assembly on November 19, Sharpe assumed, "upon mature deliberation," that the delegates had formed a bill to supply not Fort Cumberland but other troops in the field, but he learned that that was not the case.[254] Sharpe continued the rebuke by telling the delegates that the session had "already been protracted to an unusual length," suggesting it was now time to pass the bill, as with every passing day, supplying Fort Cumberland became increasingly difficult.[255]

On November 24, the lower house finally passed a bill amounting to £20,000 to support the continued defense of the colony and to support the overall war effort.[256] In passing the bill, the delegates called for the funding be raised via bills of credit and that the other half be raised through taxes on real estate. The bill was considered by the upper house on December 1 and outright rejected.[257] Even with the rejection, Sharpe continued to urge the delegates to pass a supply bill. The rejected bill and continued urging to pass a new one caused the delegates to defend their actions by lashing out at Sharpe. Their defense came as a result of an accusation that they were not fully supporting the war effort. In responding to Sharpe's continued and seemingly relentless calls for more funding, the delegates felt that they had put forth the best bill possible and that "upon the most mature deliberation, we cannot see how we can make a better provision for the ease, satisfaction, and quiet of the Back inhabitants, that has been already done by the bill sent by us to the upper house, and by them rejected."[258] The session ended without additional funding, and Sharpe blamed the lower house, stating they had "purposely crowded the bill with everything that tended to cramp the service....The upper house rejected it without hesitation & the burgesses would not...be prevailed on to frame any other bill whatever."[259] In preparation for the potential dissolution of the Maryland forces, Sharpe ordered four companies of militia to make preparations to replace them.

The year 1757 came to a close with Sharpe lamenting the inability of the lower house to create a bill that met the requirements he had received from the earl of Loudoun. Sharpe explained in a letter to Lord Baltimore, the proprietor of Maryland, Frederick Calvert, that the lower house did not provide for garrisoning Fort Cumberland, specifically mentioning that he believed the lower house's refusal to act as "a most violent attack on his Majesty's prerogative."[260] Sharpe continued that he had "been a long time convinced that nothing effectual can be done in America unless all the Colonies compelled to furnish their respective Quotas towards carrying on an offensive war, & I think the conduct of our Assembly…will shew [sic] that nothing is to be expected from them without compulsion."[261] The only consolation that Sharpe had was his ability to call out the militia, since he had "ample power & authority" to do so, and impress on the citizens of the colony to support the militia if the Maryland forces were disbanded in the near future.[262] By the end of January 1758, the assembly was again called into session. This time, Sharpe had the direct support of Loudoun. In the aftermath of the previous session's failure, Sharpe sent a copy of the bill to Loudoun to inspect. After reading the bill, Loudoun concluded that the law, if it were passed, was a "direct infringement upon the King's undoubted prerogative," due to the delegates' refusal to allow Maryland troops to operate outside of the colony's borders.[263] With Loudoun's opinion in hand, Sharpe again pursued additional funding at the next session.

Calling the assembly into session on February 6, 1758, Sharpe wasted little time in stating his goals for the session. He put before the assembly the letter from Loudoun that expressed Loudoun's opinion of the last session with the hope that the delegates "will not…disappoint him in the hopes… that your care for the preservation of the lives and properties of your fellow subjects, your zeal for the common cause, and your duty to the king will induce you to grant the supplies."[264] In response, the delegates requested an explanation regarding a specific phrase that called for the act to not only follow the instructions given but also be "agreeable to our happy Constitution of Government in the British Dominions."[265] The clarification requested by the delegates was likely regarding the supremacy of the king's ability to order his military forces, including those of its colonies, to go where they were needed. Loudoun and Sharpe believed that the king had the absolute right to order those fighting in his forces to march where needed, including those provincial forces fighting outside the colony from which they were raised. Sharpe, unsure of Loudoun's meaning in his letter, explained that it was likely regarding colonial attempts to restrain the service of some of the troops, keeping them to protect their own colonies instead of fighting for the common good.[266]

The funding bill Sharpe requested, however, did not become the priority of the delegates. Specifically, the delegates focused on why Sharpe called out two companies of militia on the frontier. Addressing Sharpe in late February, the delegates questioned the need for two militia companies to be called into service and also requested that the governor provide them with all orders issued related to these militia companies.[267] The delegates were attempting to enact a form of oversight over the actions Sharpe had taken regarding the militia. It was a power that the delegates had little standing to take, since Sharpe, as governor, was also commander in chief of the forces called into Maryland's service. However, instead of causing a stir, Sharpe explained that he had acted preemptively in calling out the militia to provide protection to the frontier in case the Maryland forces were disbanded.[268]

On February 24, 1758, Sharpe appeared before both houses of the assembly to present Loudoun's plans for a spring campaign. Loudoun again called for additional troops to be raised to put his plan into action. This time, those troops that were raised were to be supplied by the king from the time they enter into royal service until the campaign's conclusion.[269] By bringing provincial soldiers into the king's pay, it was believed that it would be much easier to get a supply bill passed. The following day, the lower house resolved to raise £10,000 to support a force of four hundred men for service with British regulars.[270] Unfortunately, for myriad reasons, this resolution did not become reality. The lower house constantly shifted the number of troops to be raised and searched for methods to acquire funding that resulted in another bill that was undoubtedly going to be rejected by the upper house. In frustration, Sharpe dismissed the assembly after only a month. Explaining the situation to Lord Baltimore, Frederick Calvert, a frustrated Sharpe wrote that a bill had been prepared, "but as the majority of the House were entirely adverse to giving money great care was taken to clog it in such a manner as might lay the upper house under the necessity of refusing it."[271]

The assembly was not out of session for long. Just weeks later, Sharpe called them back into session. The British commander in North America had changed yet again. Now in command was Major General James Abercromby, and under the direction of William Pitt, the newly appointed secretary of state for the Southern Department, plans changed, especially the way the British related to their provincial counterparts.[272] Now, instead of setting quotas and forcing colonial assemblies to pass supply bills, Pitt ordered Abercromby to request the colonies raise as many men as possible, with the caveat being that those men were going to be supplied and equipped by Great Britain, with reimbursement possible for other expenses accrued by the colonies.[273] This new directive should have made it much easier for Sharpe to get support from the Maryland delegates.

Relaying the new instructions, Sharpe advised the assembly that a meeting a quota was no longer expected. Instead, Maryland, along with Virginia and Pennsylvania, was to provide a portion of an army under the command of Brigadier General John Forbes.[274] In return for supplying and equipping the provincial force, the respective colonies were expected to raise, clothe and pay their forces, with the expectation that the colonies would be reimbursed based on how active they were to answer the call.[275] With these new stipulations, the lower house quickly began forming a bill after resolving to raise an additional £40,000 for the war effort.[276]

While the lower house debated the new bill, it returned to the issue with the militia raised during the previous session. Sharpe had preemptively called out two militia companies to defend the frontier in case the regular Maryland forces were disbanded. In the current session, the delegates asked for an additional explanation, inquiring why another militia company was mustered and what law or authority had allowed Sharpe to do so.[277] The delegates were challenging Sharpe's authority to call on the militia in a time of need due to the need to pay for those militia troops. As if he needed to explain, Sharpe told the delegates that he believed the law passed in September 1756 allowed for the provisioning of the militia companies called into service and that the law was still in effect. Not only that, Sharpe had specifically requested that the law he cited exempted certain militia companies from being called out.[278]

While wrangling with the governor over his ability and authority to call out the militia, the delegates diligently worked on the new supply bill. Taking time to develop different aspects of the bill, by mid-April, the lower house passed a bill granting £45,000 for service to the king and the defense of the frontier, with £35,000 being issued in bills of credit.[279] To do so, they intended to raise taxes and pursue the proprietor's revenue sources. With the bill's passage, it was sent to the upper house to face scrutiny. Sharpe was not hopeful, writing to John St. Clair, the British quartermaster general in North America, that he believed the bill would not pass.[280] Taking the bill under consideration on April 12, the members of the upper house resolved that they could not pass the bill in its present form and returned it to the delegates without providing explanation.[281] In response, the delegates wrote a scathing response, demanding an explanation from the upper house. It wasn't the first time this had taken place, as the delegates stated "after refusing two bills… for his Majesty's Service, without mentioning objections you might have to either of them, your honours have returned a Third.…If your objections had been made to either of those or the present bill, we should have shewed [*sic*] the utmost readiness…to have brought about the passage of them."[282] All the delegates requested was guidance about the corrections needed to get the bill passed. In response, the upper house members stated that the delegates, in previous resolutions, said the upper house "had no right but to pass or reject Money Bills" and that to avoid dispute, they had simply rejected the bill without reason.[283] However, as the delegates requested, the upper house did provide its reasons. The members objected to the beginning of the bill in which the delegates "give and grant," since the bill could not pass without the consent of the proprietor and the agreement of the upper house.[284] Taxing real estate, especially land owned by the proprietor, and the house, assuming for itself the right to nominate officers, were also causes the delegates provided for not passing the bill.[285] After further objections to the role of officers and the increased taxes, especially the tax on the proprietor's quit rents (payments made directly to the proprietor) and requirements for funding certain aspects of the Maryland forces, the upper house returned the bill to the delegates.

With the war still raging on the frontier, the back and forth continued between the two houses of the assembly, as each tried to exert its will on the other. Sharpe was losing hope that a new bill would make it through the increasingly hostile legislature. Writing to Brigadier General Forbes in late April, Sharpe informed the general that the delegates of the lower house had passed the bill four times with little change but with it being rejected each time by the upper house.[286] The stalemate continued into May. In an effort to salvage the bill, Sharpe suggested to both houses the need to form a conference—much like the one that successfully passed the 1756 supply bill—to resolve the impasse.[287] The bill languished, as the two sides were in entrenched in their positions, forcing Sharpe to end the session on May 13, with the hope to bring legislature back into session after a short break.[288]

Despite the legislature's inactivity, the war continued with no end in sight. Sharpe was unhappy that yet another supply bill had failed to pass. Writing Forbes again toward the end of the session, Sharpe remarked that he had given up all hope of obtaining supplies and that he was forced to end the session.[289] By the end of May, the Maryland troops at Forts

Cumberland and Frederick were being supplied through bills of credit that the colony would eventually have to be repaid, and the men themselves, despite months of faithful service, had not been paid. To keep Maryland's troops in the field, General Forbes advised Sharpe that he would provide a sum of money in the hopes that the Marylanders would remain in the service until the conclusion of the planned campaign against Fort Duquesne, with the caveat that the assembly would repay the funding advance.[290] With this, Forbes began gathering his army in early June, ordering the Maryland forces to join the growing British army encamped near Carlisle, Pennsylvania.[291] In the coming campaign, the Marylanders, despite lacking the full support of the assembly, proved themselves. Acting as scouts and fighting in two pitched battles near Fort Duquesne in September and Fort Ligonier in October, the Marylanders performed well and suffered terribly. Forbes wrote to William Pitt, "I must commend the spirit of some of the provincials, particularly the Maryland Troops, who I retained in the Service, after being left to disband and therefore I obliged to keep them together on our pay…to enable them to carry on the service" despite being ill-prepared for the conditions they endured.[292]

Back in Maryland, Governor Sharpe called the assembly back into session for the first time since May. In opening the session, Sharpe held nothing back, as he explained that the assembly's actions in previous legislative sessions made Maryland stand out among its sister colonies and that the generals commanding in the mid-Atlantic region entertained a "very unfavourable [sic] opinion of the people of this province."[293] During this session, Sharpe wished for the assembly to repay General Forbes for advancing a line of credit to maintain Maryland's troops in the field and David Ross, the colony's commissary agent, who also advanced funds to keep Maryland's troops and militia supplied at Forts Cumberland and Frederick.[294] In response, the two houses pledged to act, but it quickly became obvious they remained entrenched in their positions from the previous session. The upper house pledged to defend the rights and privileges of the proprietor Frederick Calvert.[295] The delegates of the lower house, being duly elected by the citizens of Maryland, felt that they were the voice of the citizens, who, in their words, were "more loyal and dutiful" than those of the other colonies, and were hopeful that the differences between the houses would not repeat themselves during the current session.[296] The lower house passed resolutions to repay General Forbes for funds expended for the Maryland Troops, with additional funding to be raised for the continued service via the same taxation methods proposed in previous sessions.[297] Those methods would again focus on the income of the proprietor and lines of credit.

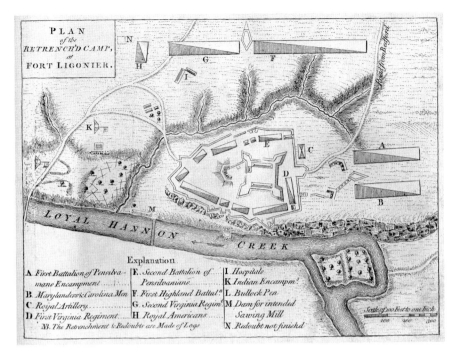

The plan of Fort Ligonier. *Massachusetts Historical Society.*

Unfortunately, the delegates were not given the chance to draft a bill. Sharpe abruptly ended the session in early November, just over a week after calling the assembly into session.[298]

After a brief interlude, Sharpe called the assembly back into session, with instructions from General Forbes on how the general believed the colony should prepare for its defense over the coming winter.[299] For this session, the lower house now must pass a bill to repay Forbes and make preparations for the defense of the colony. On November 28, the delegates passed resolutions calling for the repayment of Forbes while also providing for the support of three hundred men who were currently serving to be stationed at Fort Frederick during the coming winter.[300] While working on this bill, word arrived on December 14, 1758, that Fort Duquesne had been abandoned by the French and occupied soon after by Forbes's army.[301] Within days of Duquesne's fall, the delegates passed a supply bill totaling £36,000.[302] Despite the French being expelled from the Ohio country, the delegates were still willing to support a defensive force on the Maryland frontier. In yet another failure, the upper house considered and rejected the bill on December 18.[303] A supply bill of that size was not considered for the rest of the session. The

TAKING POSSESSION OF FORT DU QUESNE.

The capture of Fort Duquesne. *Wallach Division Picture Collection, the New York Public Library.*

session ended on Christmas Eve 1758, and the assembly failed to pass a supply bill supporting defense of the frontier—but it did manage to pass a bill that repaid Forbes.[304]

As 1758 came to a close, Maryland's frontier was relatively safe from French and Native forays. The fall of Fort Duquesne removed the primary French threat to the middle colonies and provided the Maryland Assembly with an opportunity to end the colony's involvement. At the end of December, a large portion of the Maryland forces returned to Fort Frederick. With the assembly's failure to pass a supply bill, the troops were essentially disbanded, with each soldier being provided a furlough or leave of absence until the assembly paid the troops what was owed to them.[305] Only a single company of about one hundred men remained in service, stationed at Fort Cumberland.[306] The following spring, the assembly returned and failed, yet again, to pass a supply bill. With that failure, Maryland was finished with the war.

"THE PEOPLE OF THIS PROVINCE IN GENERAL SEEM DEAD TO ALL SENSE OF GRATITUDE AND DUTY"

MARYLAND'S INACTION

The capture of Fort Duquesne in late 1758 brought a moment of relief for frontier settlements in Maryland. The primary threat to the region, Fort Duquesne, was now gone, but the war was certainly not over. The focus of military operations shifted northward, with efforts to push the French out of North America by capturing their Canadian strongholds in Quebec and Montreal. Those efforts, now overseen by the new commander of British forces in North America Jeffery Amherst, were to be supported by the British colonies, including Maryland. However, Governor Sharpe, after years of fighting with the Maryland Assembly to support the defense of the Maryland frontier, understood that those efforts were going to be next to impossible.

With the threat of Fort Duquesne removed, the situation on the frontier continued to improve. There was no longer a constant threat of French or Native attacks on frontier settlements. However, the French and their Native allies lingered in the region. The former commander of Fort Duquesne, Francois-Marie Le Marchand de Lignery, was gathering a large force to recapture the strategic location where the British were erecting the formidable Fort Pitt on the remains of the old French fort.[307] Attacks continued on the frontier, with raids taking place in the spring of 1759 in an effort to cut the supply lines between Fort Pitt and the supply bases to the east, notably those located at Fort Bedford and Fort Ligonier.[308] With the capture of Fort Duquesne, British commander in chief Jeffery Amherst

Sir Jeffery Amherst. *Library of Congress.*

wanted the colonial assemblies to continue providing support with both men and material to the war effort. The British were ready to press the French, and that effort required the colonies to take part. In Maryland, Governor Sharpe had learned that the support Amherst was requesting was not going to come easily. Writing to Amherst in late January 1759, Sharpe informed the general about how the Maryland Assembly did not fully support the Marylanders serving in the conflict and that those troops had not received any sort of payment from the colony since October 1757.[309] Continuing, Sharpe told Amherst that "within the last year I met the Assembly of this Province...several times and used my utmost endeavors to induce them to comply with the Requisitions of his Majesty's Generals," but those efforts proved to be useless.[310] Sharpe did not have any hope that the assembly would agree to any kind of support for continuing the war, and as such, the Marylanders serving were allowed to disband until the assembly could the provide payments owed them and additional new funds for maintaining the troops.[311] As the days of early 1759 grew warmer, Amherst requested that Sharpe do his best to push the assembly, including the upper house, "to exert every means in their power for collecting and forwarding" men and material required "for the support and maintenance of the King's Forces" in the coming campaign.[312] Sharpe made one last effort to push the assembly to action.

On April 4, 1759, Sharpe began his last-ditch effort to get the Maryland Assembly to continue supporting the war effort. Calling the assembly into session, Sharpe detailed the extensive efforts taken by Great Britain to protect the colonies, including Maryland. He also passed on the request and

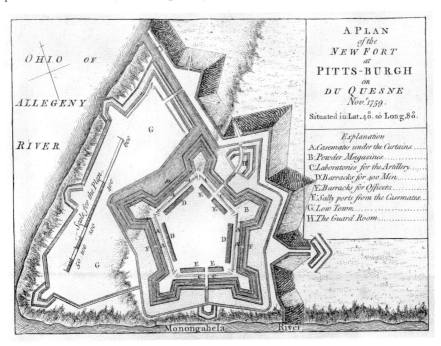

The plan of Fort Pitt. *Massachusetts Historical Society.*

expectations of Secretary of State William Pitt that each colonial assembly be urged to "raise with all possible dispatch, as large a body of men as the circumstances of each province to allow, to act in conjunction with such of the King's regular troops as may…be employed against his enemies" in North America.[313] Sharpe also provided letters from Amherst and General John Stanwix to bolster his argument to continue supporting the war effort. The delegates agreed that they would do the best they could, with the hope that the failures of the previous sessions in continuing to fund the war and those responsible would be "induced by the contents of the letters" to take the opportunity to continue funding the war.[314] They also held out hope that those responsible for those past failures could find the ability to concur with whatever proposal they presented to fulfill Sharpe's request.

The debate from the delegates did not take long. Just two days into the session, they passed, overwhelmingly, a resolution to raise and supply one thousand men to support the forces commanded by General Stanwix in the upcoming campaign to solidify the British hold on the Ohio Valley.[315] Interestingly, when the details of this resolution came up for a vote, including a bounty to be paid to men who enlisted, plus the additional resolution to raise one hundred men to act as rangers to protect the inhabitants of the western frontier, the end result was much different. The two resolutions concerning the bounty and company of rangers that were to be housed at Fort Frederick were both rejected by the delegates. Despite the rejection, the delegates resolved to continue discussing the matter.

On the following day, April 7, 1759, the delegates put forth several resolutions, including the two that had failed passage the previous day. The resolutions lowered the bounty to be offered, resolved to repay the money advanced by General Forbes the previous fall to keep the Maryland troops in the field, provided payment to those militia units that took part in the defense of the frontier and garrisoned the various forts, provided payment for the housing of British troops in three Maryland counties and set aside the funds to complete the construction of a road from Fort Frederick to Fort Cumberland.[316] These resolutions both honored the request of Sharpe and the royal officials and set up an exit for Maryland to discontinue supporting the war effort with little debt on its books. The committee formed to determine the amount and use of the funds in question and presented a ledger that resulted in a bill totaling over £50,000 sterling. After sharing their report with the lower house, the delegates sought to pass a bill for the sum of £60,000 to support British efforts and the defense of the colony by assessing taxes on "all estates, real and personal, and lucrative offices and employments."[317] Passed overwhelmingly, the resolution implied that, once again, the delegates were going to go after the proprietor by taking a cut of his funds while also taxing the estates of the proprietor. Several days passed as the delegates worked on the final details of the bill. Finally, on April 14, the bill was passed by a vote of 28–19.[318] With its passage, the bill was sent to the upper house for consideration.

Since Sharpe started his duties as the colonial governor of Maryland in 1753, any funding bills that sought to raise taxes on the proprietary to pay for the colony's needs proved to be the most contentious. With the exception of the 1756 supply bill, each of the bills previously passed by the lower house were rejected by Sharpe and the councilmen in the upper house. This bill would be no different. Taking up the bill on April 16, the six councilmen of the upper house spent little time in rejecting the bill. In rejecting the bill, the councilmen stated that in "finding it in all its Material parts the same which had in four different sessions before been sent up to and as often returned with a negative we this morning upon a single reading sent it down to you with a negative."[319] The councilmen, in rejecting the bill, provided a chance for the delegates to rework the bill, pleading with them that the time for action was quickly approaching.

Despite this overture, the rejection of the bill by the upper house was the final straw for Sharpe. In one last attempt to keep Maryland involved in supporting the war, Sharpe angrily wrote to the delegates, asking if they had resolved to any supply bill aside from the bill that had now been rejected five times, as General Stanwix was waiting for word on whether to expect support from Maryland.[320] Quickly, the delegates voted to let Sharpe know that they had not agreed to the passage of a bill to continue Maryland's support for the war. The vote, which ended hope for continued support, caused Sharpe to sharply scold the delegates. After calling the membership of the entire lower house to the chambers of the upper house, Sharpe allowed his anger at the inability of the lower house to pass a bill to boil over:

> After the Resentment you have expressed at my endeavors to remind you of, and exhort you to, the discharge of your duty, when you seemed to have lost sight of it in the too eager, and unseasonable, pursuit of other objects, and after you have explicitly resolved to admit of no propositions to provide for his Majesty's Service upon any other plan, than that, of which you have experienced the certain Impracticability in the miscarriages of the same bill five times, in as many successive sessions, I have not the least glimmering of hope, however expressive of zeal you professions have been and interesting

the occation [sic], *that you will entertain any disposition to make amends for you former failures, and therefore as a continuation of this session will only augment the very unprofitable and heavy expense you have already imposed on your constituents, a regard to their ease has determined me…to put a period to it, by proroguing this Assembly.*[321]

By ending the session, Sharpe put an end to Maryland's involvement in the war. Sharpe's disgust with the inaction of the assembly bled into letters he wrote to Amherst, Stanwix and Secretary William Pitt. Writing to Pitt, Sharpe found the results of the session to be unfortunate, since he believed the "people's representatives who compose the lower house…or at least a majority of them, came together with a fix't resolution not to propose nor agree to any other bill for raising money or troops besides that which the… upper house had four times before refused."[322] Sharpe did not expect to call the assembly back into session anytime soon. Reporting to Lord Baltimore, Frederick Calvert, Sharpe relayed to him that at the advice of the members of the governor's council, he had prorogued the assembly until July, when he expected the council would again advise him to push off the next session of the assembly.[323]

While the assembly was out of session, the fighting continued on the frontier. In the mid-Atlantic, the fighting followed the same pattern as it had in previous years. French-directed Native raids attacked various points along the frontier. These attacks included one in mid-May, when the *Maryland Gazette* reported that a sutler known by the name of Captain Wert, who kept a store at Fort Frederick while it was in operation, was killed along with three others in an attack near Loyalhannon in Pennsylvania.[324] In two other attacks, a wagon train was captured in late May by a large contingent of French and Natives, and in early July, attacks were launched against Fort Ligonier and Fort Bedford (present-day Bedford, Pennsylvania).[325] The ferocity of these attacks by the French and their Native allies proved they were still a formidable opponents. However, British and Provincial forces won major victories at Ticonderoga (July 1759), Fort Niagara (July 1759) and the Battle of Quebec (September 1759), and these victories all but ended French resistance in North America. By the time the Maryland Assembly was called back into session, the war was all but over in North America.

Even with France facing defeat in Canada, the delegates in Maryland's lower house could not be convinced to pass a suitable bill to support the effort. Opening the first session in nearly a year, Sharpe once again laid before the delegates two letters from Amherst and Pitt and called for the delegates to follow the king's call for "all his faithful and brave subjects in Maryland" to cooperate with the campaign in Canada by raising "as large a body of men, as the number and situation of our inhabitants can allow."[326] Sharpe even shared that the king's commissaries were to supply the provincial forces in the same manner as the royal troops, with the colony only to be responsible for raising the troops and paying them.[327] Despite the burden being lessened, the delegates would not pass a bill to raise and provide for troops for the Canadian campaign. Even with several amendments proposed, the two houses of the assembly could not agree on a final bill. The session ended in early April with no support bill. Writing to Amherst a day before the session ended, Sharpe reported that the delegates, in an attempt to keep up appearances, voted to raise a sizable force of one thousand men but continued seeking the funds by means that had been rejected five times previously.[328] Sharpe, in frustration, told Amherst:

> *As the people of this province in general seem dead to all sense of gratitude & duty to our most gracious Sovereign & the mother country & to have been incited at the beginning of the War to grant supplies by no other motive than Fear (our frontiers being then laid waste & depopulated by the Savages) & the inhabitants now think themselves quite secure I do not imagine their representatives will be by any means prevailed on to raise & support any more troops during the continuance of this war & I much question whether they will ever have honour enough to pay off the arrears which are due to the forces that were some time ago in the service of the province.*

Sharpe, holding the delegates and the colony as a whole in contempt, was done trying to convince them to support the war. The capture of the final French stronghold at Montreal in September 1760 ended the war in North America.

With the war in North America over, Maryland's government and citizens began to focus on internal affairs. Settlers returned to their homesteads on the frontier, while Sharpe and the assembly continued moving the colony forward and away from war. In one instance, the border dispute that had been raging between Maryland and Pennsylvania was finally settled, with commissioners being appointed by the respective colonies to work out the border's location, the soon-to-be-famous Mason-Dixon line.[329] In another, much more obvious change that proved the war was over, the governor's council advised Sharpe to lease the land on which Fort Frederick resided on

December 30, 1760.[330] With no immediate threat to Maryland, the fort was no longer needed and had been sitting mostly empty since the Maryland forces were disbanded in early 1759. In 1761, the final French outpost in Detroit surrendered to the British, officially ending the French and Indian War in North America. Peace was finally a reality along the frontiers, but a new threat would arise to once again unleash terror.

Following the British victory in North America, relations between Natives and British colonists remained in a tense and uneasy peace. Discontent slowly built among the Native tribes, particularly those tribes that resided in the Ohio country that saw promises broken and thousands of colonists flooding onto tribal lands. This discontent began in the immediate aftermath of the French defeat, when British commanding general Jeffery Amherst changed British policy. When British troops were on campaign in the Ohio Valley and took possession of French outposts, the expectation of the Native tribes in the region was that the British would abandon the posts and leave the land to the Natives. William Johnson, acting as a British agent dealing with Natives, was reminded by two tribes associated with the Iroquois that at the beginning of the war, promises were made that, that at the war's conclusion, "you would demolish all your outposts & fortifications erected in our Country."[331] Amherst, in fact, had chosen to not only retain possession of the captured French forts but strengthen their positions as well. The most evident of these was the construction of Fort Pitt on the former site of Fort Duquense, where the Alleghany and Monongahela Rivers join to form the Ohio River. Initially built to retain control of the important confluence, by 1761, Fort Pitt had expanded to cover nearly seventeen acres with a space to house a garrison of one thousand men, and it even included a village outside the walls of the fort to house several hundred civilians.[332] It was a massive site and certainly would have caused concern for the local tribes that had just recently been allied with the French and remembered the small footprint the French had maintained. In their minds, if the British were only there to fight the French, why maintain such a heavy presence?

In addition to British military forces maintaining an ever-growing presence on the frontier, colonial settlers flowed into the region. Following the official signing of a peace treaty that ended the war between France and Great Britain, trade and settlement changed drastically. First, traders arrived, and the trade goods being offered to the Natives for the furs they supplied were different. British traders were not permitted to offer rum, gunpowder, ammunition or guns. Instead, they provided trade goods that the Natives had little or no use for.[333] Concerned with this growing resentment, Johnson shared worries of Native traders with Amherst, hoping, for a short time, that the normal methods of trading with the Natives, which included gift-giving, could continue. In response, Amherst rejected the notion of normal trade and gift-giving and stated that he did not see why the British should support the Natives through gift-giving. It was Amherst's belief that the Natives should support themselves and not be bribed to continue a good relationship.[334] He also believed that the Natives should be made to barter to "keep them constantly employed by means of which they will have less time to concert, or carry into execution, any schemes prejudicial to his Majesty's interests."[335] Amherst's beliefs and approaches to the Natives west of the Appalachians would spell trouble for the frontiers of the British colonies.

Amherst's treatment of the Native tribes and the permanent nature of British forces saw a wave of settlers move onto Native lands. William Johnson wrote in October 1762 that the Natives were disgusted with how settlers yearned to settle on Native lands.[336] In droves, settlers moved from the crowded cities into the untapped lands formally claimed by the French.[337] The influx of settlers and the trade situation continued to alienate the Native tribes that were living in the area. With each passing day, it appeared to the Natives that Great Britain and its colonists were intent on pushing them off their lands. George Croghan, Johnson's assistant in dealing with Native tribes, particularly those in the Ohio region, was told by Shawnee, Seneca and Delaware tribesmen that they never intended to fight the British but that "it's full time for them to prepare to defend themselves & their country from [the British]."[338] The tensions between the British and Natives continued to rise until they reached a breaking point. When the news of peace reached the frontier in 1763, the Natives were incensed. In the peace treaty, France surrendered all its claims in Canada and the Ohio country, including land owned by Native tribes, to Great Britain.

Seeing that the British dominance was growing, Natives began to turn to each other for support and began talking about resisting British expansion. One of those Natives was Ottawa chief Pontiac. Pontiac, in the words of Ranger Robert Rogers, was a man who was "greatly honored and revered by his subjects."[339] Using his position and influenced by the teachings of Neolin, a Delaware who rejected British rule and called for resistance, Pontiac managed to pull together a confederation of Native tribes in the Great Lakes region and Ohio country to fight, with the goal of expelling the

PONTIAC.

THE GREAT CHIEF OF THE OTTAWAS, LEADER OF THE IN-
DIANS OF THE MIDDLE WEST IN THE SEVEN YEARS' WAR

Left: An artist's depiction of Chief Pontiac. *Courtesy of the Ohio History Connection.*

Below: Pontiac intended to capture Fort Detroit by meeting with Gladwin and then launching a surprise attack. *Courtesy of the Ohio History Connection.*

VISIT OF PONTIAC AND THE INDIANS TO MAJOR GLADWIN.

British from their forts and pushing the settlers off Native lands. Pontiac's plan called for the attacks on border settlements during the harvest season, with crops and animals being destroyed, settlers being killed or captured and the British forts being captured after starving the garrisons.[340] The attack began in May 1763, and by early summer, Pontiac's War had spread across the frontier. Natives captured several British forts and laid siege to the symbol of British power on the frontier, Fort Pitt. At Fort Pitt, the Delaware and Shawnee chiefs relayed to the commander of the fort why they were there: "You marched your armies into our country, and built forts here, though we told you, again and again, that we wished you to move. This land is ours, and not yours."[341]

The renewed violence on the frontiers quickly spread toward Maryland's borders. The first reports of violence on the frontier reached Annapolis in early June 1763, when the *Maryland Gazette* published an account from an officer in Pennsylvania that Natives had attacked and killed several people near Fort Pitt, attacked Fort Detroit and captured two British forts near Lake Erie.[342] Over the next several weeks, reports continued filtering in of Native attacks in Pennsylvania and Virginia that were creeping ever closer to Maryland. Finally, on July 15, 1763, Governor Sharpe received a letter from Thomas Cresap, who was living just miles from Fort Cumberland, that reported on the situation on the Maryland frontier. He reported having been attacked on three successive days by Native war parties. They attacked a work party that was preparing to harvest wheat in a field. When Cresap stumbled on a party of men at the entrance of Cresap's lane, about one hundred yards from his home, a brief firefight ensued, and several were wounded. Their last attack was on a party of men, women and children who were heading for refuge at Cresap's home; the attack resulted in two deaths and the wounding of several others. The local settlers were seeking refuge in Cresap's fortified home, and they were described by Cresap of "destitute of every necessity of life" and were "penned up & likely to be butchered without immediate relief & assistance…unless from the Province to which they belong."[343]

Sharpe, after receiving reports of the hostilities on the frontier, did what he could to defend the colony. The assembly was not currently in session, and the crisis called for Sharpe to use the powers available to him. He instructed the commanding officer of the Frederick County Militia, Colonel Thomas Prather, to prepare militia parties to begin patrolling west of South Mountain to protect the inhabitants and defend Fort Frederick, if needed, as he ordered the fort to be opened to the settlers who were living beyond

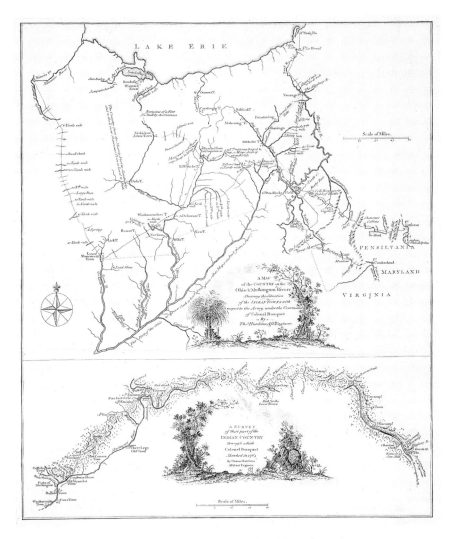

A map of the Ohio Country in 1764. *Courtesy of the Ohio History Connection.*

the fort to allow them to seek refuge there.[344] The terror on the frontier was reminiscent of the raids that had taken place just years before. In a letter published in the *Maryland Gazette*, a resident of Frederick-town wrote:

> *Every day, for some time past, has offered the melancholy scene of poor distressed families driving downwards, through this town, with their effects, who have deserted their plantations, for fear of falling into the cruel hands of our savage enemies, now daily seen in the woods. And never was panic*

Colonel Bouquet in conference with Natives at a council fire, near his camp on the banks of the Muskingum River, October 1764. *Library of Congress.*

more general or forcible than that of the back inhabitants, whose terrors, at this time, exceed what followed on the defeat of General Braddock, when the frontiers lay open to the incursions of both French and Indians. Whilst Conococheague settlement stands firm, we shall think ourselves in some sort of security from their insults here. But shoult the inhabitants there give way, you would soon see your city, and the lower counties, crowded with objects of compassion, as the flight would, in that case, become general.

Chaos once again reigned on the frontier.

Just as quickly as the raids into Maryland started, they ended. By mid-August 1763, the Natives had been driven west to what is today Ohio and Illinois. This was largely due to the British victory at the Battle of Bushy Run on August 4–5, 1763, when Henry Bouquet, leading a relief column toward Fort Pitt defeated a large force of 400 Native warriors.[345] To prevent further raids, an expedition into Ohio was needed. Bouquet and his force needed reinforcement after the Battle of Bushy Run. To take part, Captain William McClellan raised a small force of just over 40 men from Frederick County, equipped with rifles, and marched in October toward Fort Pitt.[346] This force, numbering 1,500 men, marched west in the fall of 1764 toward the Delaware and Shawnee villages.[347] Upon arrival, Bouquet made an ultimatum to the Natives: they were to release any white prisoners they held or prepare to face his army.[348] After the Natives quickly completed the request, an informal peace began on the frontier, with a formal peace treaty being agreed to in 1766.

After nearly a decade of off-and-on warfare, Maryland found itself at peace. From 1754 to 1759 and again in 1763, Marylanders answered the call to defend the colony, despite the inability of its colonial assembly to fully support their efforts. The peace gained through Bouquet's 1764 expedition and the formal peace in 1766 marked the end of an era and the beginning of another. In less than ten years, many of the Marylanders who found themselves defending the colony and the interest of the British Crown would find themselves in rebellion against their king.

6

"BUT WAR, ANYTHING, IS PREFERABLE TO A SURRENDER OF OUR RIGHTS"

THE ROAD TO REVOLUTION

The French and Indian War and the larger global war it sparked proved to be the costliest war at the time for Great Britain and its colonies. The colonies spent vast amounts of treasure to raise and supply provincial troops to act in concert with regular British forces. Together, the colonies expended over £2.5 million sterling (nearly $600 million today).[349] However, as the war dragged on, Great Britain bore the brunt of the cost, having to send a considerable number of forces, both on land and sea, to North America, and at times, it had to supply the provincial troops to convince the assemblies to grant more funding. By the end of Pontiac's War in 1766, Great Britain was looking to recover economically from the war, efforts that will spark yet another conflict in North America.

In Maryland, the cost of the war was considerably less than it was in its sister colonies. This was largely due to the infighting of the assembly. The delegates of the lower house saw it as a their right to spend funds raised from taxes in the colony, including those meant for the proprietor and the upper house, the governor's council, which was in place to protect the rights and funds of the proprietor, Frederick Calvert. Only twice during the war did the assembly pass supply bills, the largest being the 1756 bill that allowed Maryland to raise and supply several hundred troops and build the immense stone-walled Fort Frederick. This bill, totaling roughly £40,000 sterling, paled in comparison to the contributions of the Maryland's immediate neighbors, Pennsylvania and Virginia, which collectively contributed nearly

£700,000 sterling.[350] Despite the infighting, the bill that was passed kept Maryland's troops in the field for nearly two years before the inability of the assembly to pass an additional funding bill forced them into the pay of Great Britain, largely due to the need for manpower in the 1758 campaign. Maryland would repay the British Crown for the funds expended to keep the Maryland forces in the field, leaving the colony with no debt remaining once the war ended.[351]

For Great Britain, however, the country's finances were in shambles when the war ended. By the end of the conflict, Great Britain's debt had doubled from £72 million sterling to £146 million sterling.[352] The amount was staggering, and with the acquisition of new lands and the need to keep a presence there, only additions were made to the financial misery of Great Britain. To keep a sizable force of British regulars in North America to hold and defend their new lands in North America, it was estimated that £200,000 sterling would need to be raised to support the defense of Britain's North American colonies.[353] To pay for a British army to be stationed in North America, the British Parliament, for the first time, passed a tax on Britain's American colonies.

The Stamp Act of 1765 was the first direct tax passed by Parliament on the colonies.[354] The act forced colonists to pay an additional duty for the right to print newspapers, pamphlets and legal documents.[355] News of the Stamp Act arrived in the colonies and sparked almost immediate outrage. Since the end of the war and Pontiac's War in 1763 and 1764, American colonist had seen the westward expansion of the British Empire in North America as an opportunity but were prohibited by King George III's Proclamation of 1763 from settling west of the Appalachian Mountains.[356] The passage of the Stamp Act only sparked further outrage and resentment toward the policies of the British government. In Maryland, Jonas Green, the editor of the *Maryland Gazette*, published news of the act in the April 18, 1765 edition of his paper: "If the melancholy and alarming accounts, we have just heard from the northward, prove true, that an Act of Parliaments, is shortly to take place, laying a heavy and insupportable STAMP-DUTY on all American gazettes."[357] Throughout the summer, Green would publish pieces from various authors who spoke out against the Stamp Act as it was set to go into effect. By the end of August, protests against the act were at a fever pitch. At one event, a large crowd, "assertors of British American privileges," gathered in Annapolis to show their dislike for a native-born Marylander who had taken up the position as a stamp distributor.[358] Reporting it, Green printed that the crowd:

Curiously dress'd up the figure of a man, which they placed in a one-horse cart, malefactor-like, with some sheets of paper in his hands before his face. In that manner they paraded through the strees of the Town, till Noon, the bell at the same time tolling a solemn knell; then they proceed to the hill, and after giving it the Mosaic Law, at the whipping post, placed it in the pillory; from whence they took it and hung it to a gibbet there erected…and then set fire to a tar-barrel underneath, and burnt it, till it fell into the barrel.[359]

In another instance, yet another crowd, numbering in the hundreds, descended on a warehouse where, according to Green's newspaper, Zachariah Hood, the stamp collector who was burned in effigy, was storing his stamps for distribution.[360] The crowd burned the warehouse to the ground, destroying Hood's stamps and causing Hood to flee Annapolis just days later.[361]

THE STAMP ACT DENOUNCED.

A Stamp Act protest. *Library of Congress.*

Tarring and feathering was one of the most violent acts of protest used by American colonists. *Library of Congress, Prints and Photographs Division, Cartoon Prints, British.*

This kind of protest and unrest in relation to the Stamp Act was common throughout the colonies. Daniel Dulaney, a Marylander who served in upper house, seeing the unrest and reading the reasons for Parliament to pass the Stamp Act, felt the need to act. Seeing the statements that were being reprinted in the *Maryland Gazette*, which remarked that Great Britain and its colonies were not codependent of each other and that Parliament had no legislative authority over the colonies, and reading various British pamphlets that degraded the standing of the American colonies, Dulaney used his training as a lawyer to argue against the act.[362] Dulaney published a pamphlet in the *Maryland Gazette* titled *Considerations on the Propriety of Imposing Taxes in the British Colonies, For the Purpose of Raising a Revenue, by Act of Parliament*, or, as it was more simply known, *Considerations*.[363] Weaving an intricate argument according to the English constitution, Dulaney concluded that Parliament was the supreme power within the empire but that the power of taxation

An example of a stamp required by the Stamp Act of 1765. *Library of Congress.*

rested only with legislatures representing the people.[364] The only representative bodies with the power to tax the people were the colonial assemblies, and Dulaney defended this argument, stating that "it is an essential principle of the English constitution that the subject shall not be taxed without his consent."[365]

Dulaney's pamphlet was successful and was republished across the colonies—and even in London.[366] In addition to his argument against parliamentary taxing, Dulaney called for his fellow colonists to continue their constant protests and to essentially economically boycott goods manufactured in Great Britain.[367] The protests against the Stamp Act grew to include resolutions passed by each colonial assembly denouncing Parliament's unlawful tax.[368] Maryland's lower house would not weigh in on the matter until September 1765, after being out of session for nearly two years. Called into session, the delegates passed unanimous resolutions, declaring that Marylanders' rights as British subjects were secured through the 1632 charter given to the first Lord Baltimore, Cecilius Calvert.[369] In closing out their resolutions and effectively ending the session, the delegates resolved:

> *It is the unanimous opinion of this house, that the representatives of the freemen of this province…together with the other part of the legislature, have the sole right to lay taxes and imposition on the inhabitants of this province…and that the laying, imposing, leaving, and collecting, any tax on, or from the inhabitants of Maryland, under colour of any other authority, is unconstitutional, and a direct violation of the rights of the freemen of this province.*[370]

Despite the protests and political resolutions, the Stamp Act went into effect on November 1, 1765, ending practically all business and publications in Maryland.[371]

For several weeks, very little business requiring the needed stamps took place. However, in Frederick County, Maryland, the magistrates of the county dispensed with the need for stamped paper to continue business, and in celebration, the Sons of Liberty gathered to hold a funeral procession for the defeated act.[372] That simple act showed how impractical the enforcement of the tax would be. As the calendar turned to 1766, protest continued, until news arrived in early spring that the Stamp Act had been repealed by Parliament, sending the colonies into frenzy with excitement.[373] In Maryland, celebrations included toasts declaring that America's submission to Great Britain should be compatible with the colonists' constitutional liberties, and the assembly even proposed that a marble statue of William Pitt be constructed in Annapolis for his part in getting the act repealed by Parliament.[374]

The downfall of the Stamp Act did not end the unrest in the colonies. In the same instance that the Stamp Act was rescinded, Parliament declared through a declaratory act that the government of Great Britain "had, hath, and of a right ought to have, full power and authority to make laws and statutes of sufficient force and validity to bind the colonies and people of America in all cases whatsoever."[375] This particular act went largely unnoticed by Marylanders and colonists as a whole, as they still believed themselves to be citizens of the British Empire. Despite the repeal of the Stamp Act, Great Britain still had to maintain its forces in North America. In early 1767, a series of acts were passed by Parliament. What become known as the Townsend Acts, named after Charles Townsend, chancellor of the exchequer, levied new taxes on the colonists that taxed goods that were being imported into the colonies, such as glass, paper and tea.[376] These new taxes led to a boycott of British goods that were coming into the colonies, and the colonies became more organized in protesting their rights within the British Empire.

The protest movement in the colonies pressed forward, with Massachusetts leading the effort. In Maryland, the rejection of the Townsend Acts was led by the lower house of the assembly. Those efforts were almost squashed when Governor Sharpe was ordered by Lord Hillsborough, the secretary for the colonies who was acting as the messenger from the king, to have the Maryland Assembly disregard an address that was being sent through the colonies by the speaker of the Massachusetts Assembly calling for the colonial assemblies to "harmonize with each other" in protest against the new tax acts.[377] On June 20, Sharpe relayed this message to the delegates of the lower house, stating that the assembly must reject the letter from Massachusetts, as the king viewed such a letter to be "most dangerous" and "calculated to inflame the minds of his good subjects in the colonies" to rise in opposition to the authority of Parliament.[378] The delegates took the governor's plea into consideration. Two days later, in spite of the wording of Sharpe's request, the delegates responded by supporting Massachusetts's

We have received Information from *Frederick* County, that at the laft Court there, the Magiftrates taking into Confideration the bad Confefequences that would attend a Stop being put to the ordinary Courfe of Juftice, if any Notice was taken of the STAMP ACT — [which had never been legally tranfmitted to them] They in a very full Court *Unanimoufly Refolved and Ordered*, That all the Bufinefs and Procefs of that Court, fhould be transfa&ed in the ufual Manner WITHOUT STAMPS, and that fuch Proceedings fhould be good and valid. The Clerk of the Court, apprehending Damage to himfelf if he made any Entry, or iffued any Procefs without Stamped Paper, refufed to comply with the Order of the Court; upon which the Court ordered him to be committed to Prifon for Contempt. He then fubmitted and was difcharged, and proceeded on Bufinefs as Formerly.

An excerpt from the December 10, 1765 edition of the *Maryland Gazette* reporting on the Frederick County protest. *Maryland Gazette Collection, Maryland State Archives.*

petition to the king, stating that they cannot be prevailed on to hold any such letter in contempt, as it was "replete with the principles of liberty," and if the rights of the people were affected at anytime, they would "endeavor to maintain and support them."[379] Immediately, the delegates adopted a series of resolutions protesting the Townsend Acts, presenting them to Sharpe, who, in disgust, abruptly ended the session. The protest in Maryland continued, but it was not until a year later that Marylanders begin their full-fledged support of the boycott of British goods that was well underway in the northern colonies.

The strength of the united colonial protest against the Townsend Acts eventually gave these tax acts the same fate as the Stamp Act. In April 1770, news reached the colonies that after only two years, all importation duties were repealed, with the exception of the tax on tea.[380] Despite the repeal, protests within the colony continued against the importation tax on tea, even with the strength of those protests steadily declining. However, the importation of tea was still lagging to the point that tea warehouses in Great Britain were still holding large quantities of tea.[381] The relative peace that had reigned between Great Britain and its colonies was shattered when Parliament passed the Tea Act in 1773. The act authorized the East India Company, one of the most important trading companies in Great Britain, to directly sell its tea to the colonists without paying taxes.[382] This new act was viewed by the colonist as an attempt to monopolize the tea trade in America, forcing smaller merchants and traders out of business.

This new act of Parliament led to protests directly on the docks of the ports in America. Most protests remained peaceful and only kept the tea from being offloaded, forcing the ships back to Great Britain.[383] In some cases, the tea was confiscated or outright destroyed, including, most famously, in Boston, where, in December 1773, colonials disguised as Natives descended on Boston Harbor, boarded ships and threw tea into the harbor.[384] This particular protest enraged Parliament, which passed the Coercive Acts to punish and set an example of Boston and the colony of Massachusetts as a whole in early 1774.[385] In support, ninety-two delegates, many former members of the Maryland Assembly, gathered in the first of many conventions. This convention condemned the actions taken by the British Crown against Massachusetts as "cruel" and "oppressive" toward the "natural rights of the people of Massachusetts Bay," who were "now suffering in the common cause of America."[386] In addition to voicing their support, the convention called for all the colonies to meet in a general congress, the end of relations with Great Britain, subscriptions to be made for the relief of those living in Boston and declared that Maryland would end all relations with any colony that refused to support the united protest of the colonies.[387] This first Continental Congress convened in September 1774 in Philadelphia.[388]

While colonial delegates congregated in Philadelphia, yet another tea party took place in Annapolis, pushing Maryland closer and closer to open revolt against the British Crown. On October 15, 1774, the *Peggy Stewart*, a ship that was owned by Annapolis merchant Anthony Stewart, arrived carrying cargo that included over two thousand pounds of tea.[389] Stewart paid the duty on the cargo, including his tea. The nonimportation of tea had continued since the Tea Act's inception in 1768, and Stewart's payment of the tea tax aroused anger in the local populace. Stewart and his business partner Thomas Williams attempted to apologize for the error and agreed that they would allow the tea—and only the tea—to be burned.[390] That simple penance was not suitable to quell the rising anger in the crowd that had gathered before a committee that was formed to resolve the issue. A very vocal and violent minority proposed "the American discipline of tarring and feathering," while others proposed the destruction of the ship carrying the tea.[391] Eventually, Charles Carroll of Carrollton, a prominent and influential citizen living near Annapolis, advised Stewart to torch his ship in the hope that it would "deter others from the like offence" in the face of the growing

A depiction of Anthony Stewart burning the *Peggy Stewart*. *Collection of the Maryland State Archives*, The Burning of the Peggy Stewart, *Francis Blackwell Mayer (1827–1899), oil on canvas, 1896 MSA SC 1545-1111.*

patriotic movement in America.[392] Following this advice, Stewart agreed to burn his ship by his own hand. Accompanied to his ship by several witnesses, Stewart directed the crew to run the ship aground in full view of Annapolis. Once the ship was run aground, Stewart set it on fire, destroying the ship and all its cargo.[393] Just weeks later, a similar episode would take place just one hundred miles away in Hagerstown, where a local, who had taken in a single box of tea, was forced to destroy the box and suffer a gathering of people who ransacked his home.[394] By the spring of 1775, the colony of Maryland was slowly preparing itself for war. Following the end of the Continental Congress in late 1774, a second convention of delegates from the counties of Maryland called for each county to begin organizing a county militia.[395] A war was brewing, but when would the first blow be struck?

In the decade following the end of the French and Indian War in 1763, Great Britain, having to now pay to provide a permanent defense for its American colonies, imposed a series of taxes on its American colonists. Each time arguing that their constitutional rights as British citizens were being violated, the citizens and their respective colonies vehemently opposed the new taxes. In Maryland, with each new act, the citizens opposed the taxes that were passed by a legislative body that did not directly represent them. Despite this, its citizens remained loyal British subjects, only hoping to have the same equal rights as citizens in Great Britain. However, with each new tax and after witnessing the actions taken against their sister colonies by the British government, Maryland's citizens were slowly pushed toward revolution. In 1766, in a testimony before Parliament regarding the placement of British troops in the American colonies on a permanent basis, Pennsylvanian Benjamin Franklin remarked that British troops would not find themselves facing a rebellion, but "they may indeed make one."[396] On April 19, 1775, that rebellion began when British regulars and colonial militia firing on each other at Lexington and Concord. News of the battles spread quickly throughout the colonies. Writing from Philadelphia, Maryland's delegate to the Second Continental Congress, and eventual signer of the Declaration of Independence Thomas Stone said to a friend:

> We must take care to do everything which is necessary for our security and defence; not suffer ourselves to be bullied or wheedled by any deceptions, declarations, or givings out. You know my heart wishes for peace, upon the terms of security and justice to America. But war, anything, is preferable to a surrender of our rights.[397]

Stone's sentiments show how drastically American colonial society and its views toward Great Britain had changed. From 1753 to 1764, the citizens of Maryland waged war against the France and its Native allies to further Great Britain's dominions in North America, despite the inability of their colonial government to fully support the war. Just over a decade later, those same citizens, once loyal to Great Britain, found themselves in rebellion, just as Benjamin Franklin had predicted.

NOTES

Introduction

1. Edgar, *Colonial Governor in Maryland*, 28.
2. Brown, *Horatio Sharpe*, 1:208.

Chapter 1

3. "Annapolis," *Maryland Gazette*, August 16, 1753.
4. Ibid.
5. Anderson, *War That Made America*, 5.
6. Borneman, *French and Indian War*, 5–6.
7. Anderson, *War That Made America*, 5.
8. Ibid.
9. Ibid., 5–6.
10. Ibid., 7.
11. Crytzer, *War in the Peaceable Kingdom*, 22
12. Ward, *Breaking the Backcountry*, 25–26.
13. Borneman, *French and Indian War*, 13–14.
14. Ibid., 10.
15. Parkman, *Montcalm and Wolfe*, 43.
16. Ward, *Breaking the Backcountry*, 22.
17. Borneman, *French and Indian War*, 14.

18. Ibid., 15.
19. Anderson, *War that Made America*, 25.
20. Céloron de Blainville, *Expedition of Celoron*, 27.
21. Ibid.
22. Ibid., 28.
23. Borneman, *French and Indian War*, 17.
24. Ward, *Breaking the Backcountry*, 26.
25. Bailey, *Ohio Company of Virginia*, 27.
26. Powell, *Forgotten Heroes*, 5.
27. Ibid., 9.
28. Powell, *Maryland*, 7.
29. Ibid., 10.
30. Powell, *Forgotten Heroes*, 28.
31. Ward, *Breaking the Backcountry*, 27.
32. Ibid., 28.
33. Ibid.
34. O'Meara, *Guns at the Forks*, 22.
35. Brown, *Horatio Sharpe*, 1:4.
36. Anderson, *War That Made America*, 39.
37. O'Meara, *Guns at the Forks*, 5.
38. Ibid., 7.
39. Ibid., 33.
40. Brown, *Horatio Sharpe*, 1:33.

Chapter 2

41. Land, *Colonial Maryland*, 5–6.
42. Ibid., 34.
43. Everstine, "Establishment of Legislative Power," 102.
44. Land, *Colonial Maryland*, 36.
45. Ibid., 37–38.
46. Ibid., 93.
47. Black, "Maryland's Attitude," 14.
48. Archives of Maryland, "Votes and Proceedings, October 2, 1753–November 17, 1753." (Hereafter cited as "Proceedings of the Lower House.")
49. Land, *Colonial Maryland*, 38.
50. Archives of Maryland, "Proceedings of the Lower House, October 31, 1753."

51. Archives of Maryland, "Proceedings of the Lower House, November 17, 1753."

52. Brown, *Horatio Sharpe*, 1:4.

53. Archives of Maryland, "Proceedings of the Lower House, November 5, 1753."

54. Ibid.

55. Archives of Maryland, "Proceedings of the Lower House, November 16, 1753."

56. Ibid.

57. Brown, *Horatio Sharpe*, 1:12.

58. Ibid., 1:10.

59. Ibid.

60. Washington, "Journey to the French Commandant."

61. Dinwiddie, *Official Records*, 73–75.

62. "Speech of the Honourable Robert Dinwiddie, Esq.," *Maryland Gazette*.

63. "Annapolis," *Maryland Gazette*, January 24, 1754.

64. "Annapolis," *Maryland Gazette*, February 7, 1754.

65. Brown, *Horatio Sharpe*, 1:33.

66. Ibid.

67. Ibid., 1:34.

68. "Annapolis," *Maryland Gazette*, February 7, 1754.

69. Archives of Maryland, "Votes and Proceedings, February 26, 1754 to March 9, 1754." (Hereafter cited as "Proceedings of the Lower House.")

70. Ibid.

71. Pleasants, *Proceedings and Acts, 1752–1754*, 411–13.

72. Ibid., 412.

73. Ibid.

74. Ibid.

75. Archives of Maryland, "Proceedings of the Lower House, February 27, 1754."

76. Archives of Maryland, "Proceedings of the Lower House, February 28, 1754."

77. Ibid.

78. Dinwiddie, *Official Records*, 105.

79. Ibid.

80. Ibid.

81. Archives of Maryland, "Proceedings of the Lower House, March 2, 1754."

82. Archives of Maryland, "Proceedings of the Lower House, March 5, 1754."

83. Archives of Maryland, "Proceedings of the Lower House, March 6, 1754," 10.
84. Ibid.
85. Archives of Maryland, "Proceedings of the Lower House, March 8, 1754," 14.
86. Ibid.
87. Archives of Maryland, "Proceedings of the Lower House, March 9, 1754," 18.
88. Anderson, *War That Made America*, 46–48.
89. Ibid.
90. Archives of Maryland, "Votes and Proceedings, May 8–30, 1754," 2. (Hereafter cited as "Proceedings of the Lower House.")
91. Ibid.
92. Archives of Maryland, "Proceedings of the Lower House, May 15, 1754," 9.
93. Archives of Maryland, "Proceedings of the Lower House, May 25, 1754," 22.
94. Ibid., 23.
95. "Annapolis," *Maryland Gazette*, June 13, 1754.
96. Ibid.
97. Archives of Maryland, "Votes and Proceedings, July 17–25, 1754," 2. (Hereafter cited as "Proceedings of the Lower House.")
98. Ibid.
99. Ibid.
100. Archives of Maryland, "Proceedings of the Lower House, July 20, 1754."
101. Pleasants, "Proceedings of the Upper House," 50:538–39.
102. Brown, *Horatio Sharpe*, 1:73.
103. Ibid., 1:77.
104. Ibid.
105. Ibid., 1:79.
106. Ibid., 1:105.
107. Ibid., 1:120–24.
108. Ibid., 1:173–74.
109. Ibid.
110. Ibid., 1:125–26.
111. Ibid., 1:127.
112. Edgar, *Colonial Governor in Maryland*, 29.
113. Archives of Maryland, "Votes and Proceedings, December 12–24, 1754," 2.

114. Ibid.

115. Ibid., 3.

116. Brown, *Horatio Sharpe*, 1:165.

117. O'Meara, *Guns at the Forks*, 111.

118. Archives of Maryland, "Votes and Proceedings, February 22 to March 26, 1755," 2. (Hereafter cited as "Proceedings of the Lower House.")

119. Brown, *Horatio Sharpe*, 1:160.

120. Pleasants, "Proceedings of the Lower House," 52:52.

121. Ibid.

122. Archives of Maryland, "Proceedings of the Lower House, March 1, 1755," 10.

123. Archives of Maryland, "Proceedings of the Lower House, March 10, 1755," 19.

124. Ibid.

125. Archives of Maryland, "Proceedings of the Lower House, March 14, 1755," 26.

126. Archives of Maryland, "Proceedings of the Lower House, March 25, 1755," 43.

127. Archives of Maryland, "Votes and Proceedings, June 23 to July 8, 1755," 6. (Hereafter cited as "Proceedings of the Lower House.")

128. Brown, *Horatio Sharpe*, 1:238.

129. Archives of Maryland, "Proceedings of the Lower House, June 29, 1755," 13.

Chapter 3

130. "Annapolis," *Maryland Gazette*, July 17, 1755.

131. "Annapolis," *Maryland Gazette*, July 24, 1775.

132. Borneman, *French and Indian War*, 69.

133. Brown, *Correspondence of Governor*, 1:257.

134. Ibid., 1:259.

135. "Annapolis," *Maryland Gazette*, August 14, 1755.

136. Brown, *Correspondence of Governor*, 1:268.

137. Ibid., 1:292.

138. Powell, *Maryland*, 78.

139. Banvard, *Tragic Scenes*, 162.

140. Ibid.

141. Brown, *Correspondence of Governor*, 1:300.

142. Ibid., 1:293.
143. "Annapolis," *Maryland Gazette*, February 26, 1756.
144. Ibid.
145. "Annapolis," *Maryland Gazette*, March 4, 1756.
146. Archives of Maryland, "Votes and Proceedings, February 23, 1756–May 22, 1756." (Hereafter cited as "Proceedings of the Lower House.")
147. Colony of Maryland, *Acts of the Province of Maryland*, 6–7.
148. Ibid.
149. Ibid., 3.
150. Archives of Maryland, "Proceedings of the Lower House, March 1, 1756," 9.
151. Ibid.
152. Archives of Maryland, "Proceedings of the Lower House, March 2, 1756," 10.
153. Ibid.
154. Ibid.
155. Ibid.
156. Ibid.
157. Nye, "Pounds Sterling to Dollars."
158. Archives of Maryland, "Proceedings of the Lower House, March 11, 1756."
159. Ibid.
160. Brown, *Horatio Sharpe*, 1:346.
161. Ibid., 1:350.
162. Ibid., 1:351.
163. Ibid.
164. Ibid.
165. Archives of Maryland, "Proceedings of the Lower House, March 27, 1756," 29.
166. Archives of Maryland, "Proceedings of the Lower House, March 31, 1756," 31.
167. Archives of Maryland, "Proceedings of the Lower House, March 30, 1756," 30.
168. Archives of Maryland, "Proceedings of the Lower House, April 1, 1756."
169. "Annapolis," *Maryland Gazette*, April 29, 1756.
170. Pleasants, "Proceedings of the Upper House of Assembly," 55:250.
171. Ibid.
172. Ibid.

173. Ibid.

174. Ibid.

175. Beverley W. Bond Jr., "The Quit-Rent System in the American Colonies," *American Historical Review* 17, no. 3 (April 1912): 496–97, https://www.jstor.org/stable/pdf/1834386.pdf.

176. Black, "Maryland's Attitude," 49.

177. Archives of Maryland, "Proceedings of the Lower House, April 16, 1756."

178. Ibid.

179. Ibid.

180. Brown, *Horatio Sharpe*, 1:389.

181. Ibid., 1:390.

182. Ibid., 1:391.

183. Archives of Maryland, "Proceedings of the Lower House, April 17, 1756."

184. Pleasants, "Proceedings of the Upper House of Assembly," 55:257.

185. Ibid., 55:258.

186. Archives of Maryland, "Proceedings of the Lower House, April 22, 1756."

187. Archives of Maryland, "Proceedings of the Lower House, April 23, 1756."

188. Pleasants, "Proceedings of the Upper House of Assembly," 55:264–65.

189. Brown, *Horatio Sharpe*, 1:391.

190. Archives of Maryland, "Proceedings of the Lower House, May 4, 1756."

191. Brown, *Horatio Sharpe*, 1:414.

192. Archives of Maryland, "Proceedings of the Lower House, May 12, 1756."

193. Ibid.

194. Pleasants, "Proceedings of the Upper House of Assembly," 55:281–83.

195. Brown, *Horatio Sharpe*, 1:469.

196. Ibid., 1:473.

197. Ibid., 1:486.

Chapter 4

198. Land, *Colonial Maryland*, 219.

199. Ibid.

200. Anderson, *War That Made America*, 97–99.

201. Brown, *Horatio Sharpe*, 1:531.

202. Ibid.

203. Ibid., 1:520–23, 534.

204. Ibid., 1:524.

205. Ibid.

206. Archives of Maryland, "*Votes and Proceedings*, April 8, 1757–May 9, 1757," 1. (Hereafter cited as "Proceedings of the Lower House.")
207. Archives of Maryland, "Proceedings of the Lower House," 2.
208. Ibid., 11.
209. Ibid.
210. Ibid.
211. Ibid.
212. Brown, *Correspondence of Governor*, 1:543.
213. Ibid.
214. Pleasants, "Proceedings of the Upper House of Assembly," 55:13–15.
215. Archives of Maryland, "Proceedings of the Lower House," 20.
216. Ibid.
217. Ibid.
218. Ibid.
219. Pleasants, "Proceedings of the Upper House of Assembly," 55:17.
220. Ibid., 55:34–37.
221. Ibid., 55:35.
222. Ibid.
223. Ibid.
224. Archives of Maryland, "Proceedings of the Lower House," 34.
225. Ibid.
226. Ibid.
227. Ibid., 37.
228. Ibid., 49.
229. Brown, *Horatio Sharpe*, 1:543.
230. Archives of Maryland, "Proceedings of the Lower House," 51.
231. Ibid., 40–41.
232. Ibid., 38.
233. Ibid.
234. Edgar, *Colonial Governor in Maryland*, 126.
235. Ibid., 130–31.
236. "Annapolis," *Maryland Gazette*, May 19, 1757.
237. O'Meara, *Guns at the Forks*, 174.
238. "Annapolis," *Maryland Gazette*, June 16, 1757.
239. "Annapolis," *Maryland Gazette*, August 4, 1757.
240. "Annapolis," *Maryland Gazette*, June, 23, 1757, *Maryland Gazette* Collection, Archives of Maryland Online, https://msa.maryland.gov/megafile/msa/speccol/sc4800/sc4872/001279/html/m1279-1164.html.

241. "Annapolis," *Maryland Gazette*, December 22, 1757.
242. Archives of Maryland, "*Votes and Proceedings*, September 28–December 16, 1757," 2. (Hereafter cited as "Proceedings of the Lower House.")
243. Archives of Maryland, "Proceedings of the Lower House," 13.
244. Ibid.
245. Archives of Maryland, "Proceedings of the Lower House, October 7, 1757," 15.
246. Archives of Maryland, "Proceedings of the Lower House, October 14, 1757," 21.
247. Archives of Maryland, "Proceedings of the Lower House, October 15, 1757."
248. Ibid.
249. Archives of Maryland, "Proceedings of the Lower House, October 19, 1757," 24.
250. Archives of Maryland, "Proceedings of the Lower House, October 21, 1757," 26.
251. Ibid.
252. Brown, *Horatio Sharpe*, 2:87.
253. Ibid., 2:85.
254. Archives of Maryland, "Proceedings of the Lower House, November 19, 1757," 46.
255. Ibid.
256. Pleasants, "Proceedings of the Upper House of Assembly," 55:172.
257. Ibid., 55:177.
258. Archives of Maryland, "Proceedings of the Lower House," 72.
259. Brown, *Correspondence of Governor*, 2:109.
260. Ibid., 2:111.
261. Ibid., 2:111–12.
262. Ibid., 2:126.
263. Ibid., 2:121.
264. Archives of Maryland, "Proceedings and Votes, February 13–March 9, 1758," 2. (Hereafter cited as "Proceedings of the Lower House.")
265. Ibid., 6.
266. Ibid.
267. Archives of Maryland, "Proceedings of the Lower House, February 23, 1758," 11.
268. Ibid., 12.
269. Ibid., 12–13.
270. Ibid., 14.

271. Brown, *Correspondence of Governor*, 2:147.
272. Anderson, *War That Made America*, 120–23.
273. Ibid., 122.
274. Archives of Maryland, "Proceedings and Votes, March 28–May 13, 1758," 2. (Hereafter cited as "Proceedings of the Lower House.")
275. Ibid.
276. Archives of Maryland, "Proceedings of the Lower House, March 31, 1758," 7–8.
277. Archives of Maryland, "Proceedings of the Lower House, April 1, 1758," 9.
278. Archives of Maryland, "Proceedings of the Lower House, April 4, 1758," 11.
279. Archives of Maryland, "Proceedings of the Lower House, April 8, 1758," 16.
280. Brown, *Correspondence of Governor*, 2:170.
281. Pleasants, "Proceedings of the Upper House of Assembly," 55:478.
282. Archives of Maryland, "Proceedings of the Lower House, April 12, 1758," 18.
283. Pleasants, "Proceedings of the Upper House of Assembly," 55:480.
284. Ibid., 55:481.
285. Ibid.
286. Brown, *Correspondence of Governor*, 2:174.
287. Archives of Maryland, "Proceedings of the Lower House, May 10, 1758," 101.
288. Ibid., 105.
289. Brown, *Correspondence of Governor*, 2:181.
290. Ibid., 2:187.
291. Ibid., 2:198.
292. Forbes, *Writings*, 239.
293. Archives of Maryland, "Proceedings and Votes, October 23–November 4, 1758," 2. (Hereafter cited as "Proceedings of the Lower House.")
294. Ibid.
295. Pleasants, "Proceedings of the Upper House of Assembly," 56:8.
296. Archives of Maryland, "Proceedings of the Lower House, October 26, 1758," 8.
297. Archives of Maryland, "Proceedings of the Lower House, October 28, 1758," 10.
298. Archives of Maryland, "Proceedings of the Lower House, November 4, 1758," 14.

299. Archives of Maryland, "Proceedings and Votes of the Lower House of Assembly of the Province of Maryland, November 22, 1758–December 24, 1758," Early State Records Online, Maryland State Archives, 18, http://aomol.msa.maryland.gov/megafile/msa/speccol/sc4800/sc4872/003195/html/m3195-1454.html. (Hereafter cited as "Proceedings of the Lower House.")

300. Archives of Maryland, "Proceedings of the Lower House, November 28, 1958."

301. Archives of Maryland, "Proceedings of the Lower House, December 14, 1758."

302. Archives of Maryland, "Proceedings of the Lower House, December 16, 1758," 41.

303. Pleasants, "Proceedings of the Upper House of Assembly," 55:54.

304. Ibid., 55:136.

305. Brown, *Correspondence of Governor*, 2:319.

306. Ibid.

Chapter 5

307. O'Meara, *Guns at the Forks*, 216.

308. Ibid.

309. Brown, *Horatio Sharpe*, 2:321.

310. Ibid.

311. Ibid., 2:322.

312. Ibid., 2:324.

313. Archives of Maryland, "*Votes and Proceedings of The Lower House of Assembly of the Province of Maryland*, April 4–17, 1759," Early State Records Online, Maryland State Archives, 58, https://msa.maryland.gov/megafile/msa/speccol/sc4800/sc4872/003195/html/m3195-1491.html. (Hereafter cited as "Proceedings of the Lower House.")

314. Archives of Maryland, "Proceedings of the Lower House," 59.

315. Ibid., 61.

316. Ibid., 62.

317. Ibid., 64.

318. Ibid., 71.

319. Pleasants, "Proceedings of the Upper House of Assembly," 55:153.

320. Archives of Maryland, "Proceedings of the Lower House," 76.

321. Ibid.

322. Brown, *Correspondence of Governor*, 2:334.

323. Ibid., 2:337.

324. "Annapolis," *Maryland Gazette*, May 24, 1759.

325. "Annapolis," *Maryland Gazette*, May 31, 1759; "Annapolis," *Maryland Gazette*, July 19, 1759.

326. Archives of Maryland, "*Votes and Proceedings*, March 22–April 11, 1760," 78.

327. Ibid.

328. Archives of Maryland, *Correspondence*, 393.

329. Powell, *Maryland*, 182.

330. Brown, *Proceedings of the Council*, 31:418.

331. Ward, *Breaking the Backcountry*, 202.

332. Ibid.

333. Fowler, *Empires at War*, 273–74.

334. Ibid.

335. Anderson, *War That Made America*, 233.

336. Calloway, *Scratch of a Pen*, 52.

337. Morgan, *Wilderness at Dawn*, 339.

338. Calloway, *Scratch of a Pen*, 67.

339. Fowler, *Empires at War*, 275.

340. Scharf, *History of Western Maryland*, 99.

341. Calloway, *Scratch of a Pen*, 72.

342. "Annapolis," *Maryland Gazette*, June 9, 1763.

343. Brown, *Correspondence of Governor*, 3:104.

344. Brown, *Proceedings of the Council*, 32:60.

345. Ward, *Breaking the Backcountry*, 229–30.

346. Land, *Colonial Maryland*, 242.

347. Powell, *Maryland*, 204.

348. Ibid.

Chapter 6

349. Wicker, "Colonial Monetary Standards Contrasted," 877.

350. Ibid.

351. Ibid., 874.

352. Anderson, *War That Made America*, 243.

353. Ferling, *Almost a Miracle*, 22.

354. Ibid.

355. Land, *Colonial Maryland*, 246.

356. Calloway, *Scratch of a Pen*, 92.

357. "Annapolis," *Maryland Gazette*, April 18, 1765.

358. "Annapolis," *Maryland Gazette*, August 29, 1765.

359. Ibid.

360. Land, *Colonial Maryland*, 247.

361. Ibid.

362. Morgan and Morgan, *Stamp Act Crisis*, 82–83.

363. Land, *Colonial Maryland*, 247.

364. Morgan and Morgan, *Stamp Act Crisis*, 85.

365. Dulany, *Considerations*, 5.

366. Land, *Colonial Maryland*, 248.

367. Ibid.

368. Morgan and Morgan, *Stamp Act Crisis*, 119.

369. McSherry, *History of Maryland*, 155.

370. Archives of Maryland, "Votes and Proceedings of the Lower House of the Province of Maryland, September 23–28, 1765," Early State Records Online, Maryland State Archives, 10, https://msa.maryland.gov/megafile/msa/speccol/sc4800/sc4872/003195/html/m3195-1917.html.

371. Land, *Colonial Maryland*, 249.

372. "Annapolis," *Maryland Gazette*, December 10, 1765.

373. Anderson, *War That Made America*, 247.

374. Land, *Colonial Maryland*, 250.

375. Anderson, *War That Made America*, 247.

376. Ibid., 259.

377. Brown, *Correspondence of Governor*, 3:492.

378. Archives of Maryland, "Votes and Proceedings, May 24–June 22, 1768," 196. (Hereafter cited as "Proceedings of the Lower House.")

379. Archives of Maryland, "Proceedings of the Lower House," 203.

380. McSherry, *History of Maryland*, 166.

381. Ibid., 172.
382. Morton, *American Revolution*, 31.
383. Morgan, *Wilderness at Dawn*, 365.
384. Morton, *American Revolution*, 31.
385. Ferling, *Almost a Miracle*, 25–26.
386. Land, *Colonial Maryland*, 300.
387. McSherry, *History of Maryland*, 173.
388. Scharf, *History of Western Maryland*, 127.
389. Land, *Colonial Maryland*, 301.
390. McSherry, *History of Maryland*, 174.
391. Land, *Colonial Maryland*, 303.
392. Hoffman, *Princes of Ireland*, 299.
393. Land, *Colonial Maryland*, 303.
394. McSherry, *History of Maryland*, 174.
395. Scharf, *History of Western Maryland*, 128.
396. Ferling, *Almost a Miracle*, 23.
397. American Archives, "Thomas Stone to Daniel."

SELECTED BIBLIOGRAPHY

Primary Sources

American Archives. "Thomas Stone to Daniel of St. Thomas Jenifer, April 24, 1776." Northern Illinois University Digital Library. https://digital.lib. niu.edu/islandora/object/niu-amarch%3A99491.

Archives of Maryland. "Commission of Horatio Sharpe as Lt. Colonel of the West Indies." Parchment MSA SC 371-1-13.

———. "Votes and Proceedings of the Lower House of Assembly of the Province of Maryland, October 2, 1753–November 17, 1753." Early State Records Online, MSA SC M 3195, Maryland State Archives. http://aomol.msa.maryland.gov/megafile/msa/speccol/sc4800/ sc4872/003195/html/m3195-0741.html.

———. "Votes and Proceedings of the Lower House of Assembly of the Province of Maryland, February 26, 1754 to March 9, 1754." Early State Records Online, Maryland State Archives. https://msa.maryland.gov/ megafile/msa/speccol/sc4800/sc4872/003195/html/m3195-0824. html.

———. "Votes and Proceedings of the Lower House of the Province of Maryland, May 8–30, 1754." Early State Records Online, MSA SC M3195, Maryland State Archives. https://msa.maryland.gov/megafile/ msa/speccol/sc4800/sc4872/003195/html/m3195-0845.html.

———. "Votes and Proceedings of the Lower House of the Province of Maryland, July 17–25, 1754." Early State Records Online, MSA SC

M3195, Maryland State Archives. https://msa.maryland.gov/megafile/msa/speccol/sc4800/sc4872/003195/html/m3195-0885.html.

———. "Votes and Proceedings of the Lower House of the Province of Maryland, December 12–24, 1754." Early State Records Online, MSA SC M3195, Maryland State Archives. https://msa.maryland.gov/megafile/msa/speccol/sc4800/sc4872/003195/html/m3195-0899.html.

———. "Votes and Proceedings of the Lower House of the Province of Maryland, February 22–March 26, 1755." Early State Records Online, MSA SC M3195, Maryland State Archives. https://msa.maryland.gov/megafile/msa/speccol/sc4800/sc4872/003195/html/m3195-0899.html.

———. "Votes and Proceedings of the Lower House of the Province of Maryland, June 23–July 8, 1755." Early State Records Online, MSA SC M3195, Maryland State Archives. https://msa.maryland.gov/megafile/msa/speccol/sc4800/sc4872/003195/html/m3195-0971.html.

———. "Votes and Proceedings of the Lower House of Assembly of the Province of Maryland, February 23, 1756–May 22, 1756." Early State Records Online, MSA SC M3195, Maryland State Archives. https://msa.maryland.gov/megafile/msa/speccol/sc4800/sc4872/003195/html/m3195-1015.html.

———. "Votes and Proceedings of the Lower House of Assembly of the Province of Maryland, April 8, 1757–May 9, 1757." Early State Records Online, Maryland State Archives. https://msa.maryland.gov/megafile/msa/speccol/sc4800/sc4872/003195/html/m3195-1149.html.

———. "Votes and Proceedings of the Lower House of Assembly of the Province of Maryland, September 28–December 16, 1757." Early State Records Online, Maryland State Archives. https://msa.maryland.gov/megafile/msa/speccol/sc4800/sc4872/003195/html/m3195-1201.html.

———. "Votes and Proceedings of the Lower House of Assembly of the Province of Maryland, February 13–March 9, 1758." Early State Records Online, Maryland State Archives. https://msa.maryland.gov/megafile/msa/speccol/sc4800/sc4872/003195/html/m3195-1307.html

———. "Votes and Proceedings of the Lower House of Assembly of the Province of Maryland, March 28–May 13, 1758." Early State Records Online, Maryland State Archives. https://msa.maryland.gov/megafile/msa/speccol/sc4800/sc4872/003195/html/m3195-1331.html.

———. "Votes and Proceedings of the Lower House of Assembly of the Province of Maryland, October 23–November 4, 1758." Early State Records Online, Maryland State Archives. https://msa.maryland.

gov/megafile/msa/speccol/sc4800/sc4872/003195/html/m3195-1438.html.

———. "Votes and Proceedings of the Lower House of Assembly of the Province of Maryland, March 22–April 11, 1760." Early State Records Online, Maryland State Archives. https://msa.maryland.gov/megafile/msa/speccol/sc4800/sc4872/003195/html/m3195-1510.html.

———. "Votes and Proceedings of the Lower House of the Province of Maryland, May 24–June 22, 1768." Early State Records Online, Maryland State Archives. https://msa.maryland.gov/megafile/msa/speccol/sc4800/sc4872/003196/html/m3196-0089.html.

Bradford, William. "This Is the Place to Affix the Stamp." *Pennsylvania Journal and Weekly Advertiser*, October 24, 1765. Library of Congress Microform Reading Room Washington, D.C. www.loc.gov/item/2004672606/.

Brown, William H., ed. *Correspondence of Horatio Sharpe*. Vol. 1, *1753–1757*. Baltimore: Maryland Historical Society, 1888. https://msa.maryland.gov/megafile/msa/speccol/sc2900/sc2908/000001/000006/html/am6p--1.html.

———. *Correspondence of Horatio Sharpe*. Vol. 2, *1757–1761*. Baltimore: Maryland Historical Society, 1890. https://msa.maryland.gov/megafile/msa/speccol/sc2900/sc2908/000001/000009/html/am9p--1.html.

———. *Correspondence of Governor Horatio Sharpe*. Vol. 3, *1761–1771*. Baltimore: Maryland Historical Society, 1895. https://msa.maryland.gov/megafile/msa/speccol/sc2900/sc2908/000001/000014/html/am14p--1.html.

———. *Proceedings of the Council of Maryland*. Vol. 31, *August 10, 1753–March 20, 1761; Letters to Governor Sharpe, 1754–1765*. Baltimore: Maryland Historical Society, 1911. https://msa.maryland.gov/megafile/msa/speccol/sc2900/sc2908/000001/000031/html/index.html.

———. *Proceedings of the Council of Maryland*. Vol. 32, *April 5, 1761–September 16, 1770*. Baltimore: Maryland Historical Society, 1913. https://msa.maryland.gov/megafile/msa/speccol/sc2900/sc2908/000001/000032/html/index.html.

Céloron de Blainville, Captain Pierre-Joseph. *Expedition of Celoron to the Ohio County in 1739*. Edited by Charles B. Galbreath. Columbus, OH: F.J. Heer Printing Co., 1921.

Chief Pontiac Portrait. Drawing, c. 1760. Pontiac Collection, Ohio History Connection.

Colony of Maryland. *Acts of the Province of Maryland at a Session of Assembly, Begun and Held at the City of Annapolis, on Monday the Twenty-Third Day of June, in the Fifth Year of the Dominion of the Right Honourable Frederick, Lord Baron of*

Baltimore, Absolute Lord and Proprietary of the Provinces of Maryland and Avalon, Etc. Annapolis: Jonas Green, 1755. Early State Records Online, MSA SC M3179, Maryland State Archives. https://msa.maryland.gov/megafile/ msa/speccol/sc4800/sc4872/003179/html/m3179-0982.html.

Dinwiddie, Robert. *The Official Records of Robert Dinwiddie, Lieutenant Governor of the Colony of Virginia, 1751–1758.* Vol. 1. Edited by R.A. Brock. Richmond: Virginia Historical Society, 1883. https://hdl.handle. net/2027/yale.39002004128626.

Dulany, Daniel. *Considerations on the Propriety of Imposing Taxes in the British Colonies, For the Purpose of Raising a Revenue, by Act of Parliament.* London: J. Almon, 1765. https://collections.lib.utah.edu/ark:/87278/s64x97gn/1307113.

Firm, John Bennett, and Robert Sayer. *The Bostonian's Paying the Excise-Man, or Tarring & Feathering.* Print, 1774. Library of Congress Prints and Photographs Division, Washington, D.C. https://www.loc.gov/ item/2004673302/

Forbes, John. *Writings of General John Forbes Relating to His Service in North America.* Edited by Alfred Proctor James. Menasha, WI: Collegiate Press, 1938. https://hdl.handle.net/2027/mdp.39015027041345.

Hutchins, Thomas. *Ohio County Map.* Columbus: Ohio History Connection Archives/Library, c. 1766.

Maryland Gazette. "Annapolis." August 16, 1753. *Maryland Gazette* Collection, MSA SC 2731, Archives of Maryland Online. https://msa.maryland. gov/megafile/msa/speccol/sc4800/sc4872/001279/html/m1279-0351.html.

———. "Annapolis." January 24, 1754. *Maryland Gazette* Collection, Archives of Maryland Online. https://msa.maryland.gov/megafile/msa/speccol/ sc4800/sc4872/001279/html/m1279-0435.html.

———. "Annapolis." February 7, 1754. *Maryland Gazette* Collection, Archives of Maryland Online. https://msa.maryland.gov/megafile/msa/speccol/ sc4800/sc4872/001279/html/m1279-0439.html.

———. "Annapolis." June 13, 1754. *Maryland Gazette* Collection, Archives of Maryland Online. https://msa.maryland.gov/megafile/msa/speccol/ sc4800/sc4872/001279/html/m1279-0514.html.

———. "Annapolis." July 17, 1755. *Maryland Gazette* Collection, Archives of Maryland Online. https://msa.maryland.gov/megafile/msa/speccol/ sc4800/sc4872/001279/html/m1279-0747.html.

———. "Annapolis." July 24, 1775. *Maryland Gazette* Collection, Archives of Maryland Online. https://msa.maryland.gov/megafile/msa/speccol/ sc4800/sc4872/001279/html/m1279-0752.html.

————. "Annapolis." August 14, 1755. *Maryland Gazette* Collection, Archives of Maryland Online. https://msa.maryland.gov/megafile/msa/speccol/sc4800/sc4872/001279/html/m1279-0763.html.

————. "Annapolis." February 26, 1756. *Maryland Gazette* Collection, Archives of Maryland Online. https://msa.maryland.gov/megafile/msa/speccol/sc4800/sc4872/001279/html/m1279-0881.html.

————. "Annapolis." March 4, 1756. *Maryland Gazette* Collection, Archives of Maryland Online. https://msa.maryland.gov/megafile/msa/speccol/sc4800/sc4872/001279/html/m1279-0886.html.

————. "Annapolis." April 29, 1756. *Maryland Gazette* Collection, Archives of Maryland Online. https://msa.maryland.gov/megafile/msa/speccol/sc4800/sc4872/001279/html/m1279-0918.html.

————. "Annapolis." May 19, 1757. *Maryland Gazette* Collection, Archives of Maryland Online. https://msa.maryland.gov/megafile/msa/speccol/sc4800/sc4872/001279/html/m1279-1144.html.

————. "Annapolis." June 16, 1757. *Maryland Gazette* Collection, Archives of Maryland Online. https://msa.maryland.gov/megafile/msa/speccol/sc4800/sc4872/001279/html/m1279-1160.html.

————. "Annapolis." June 23, 1757. *Maryland Gazette* Collection, Archives of Maryland Online. https://msa.maryland.gov/megafile/msa/speccol/sc4800/sc4872/001279/html/m1279-1164.html.

————. "Annapolis." August 4, 1757. *Maryland Gazette* Collection, Archives of Maryland Online. https://msa.maryland.gov/megafile/msa/speccol/sc4800/sc4872/001279/html/m1279-1188.html.

————. "Annapolis." December 22, 1757. *Maryland Gazette* Collection, Archives of Maryland Online. https://msa.maryland.gov/megafile/msa/speccol/sc4800/sc4872/001279/html/m1279-1276.html.

————. "Annapolis." May 24, 1759. *Maryland Gazette* Collection, Archives of Maryland Online, MSA SC 2731. https://msa.maryland.gov/megafile/msa/speccol/sc4800/sc4872/001280/html/m1280-0125.html.

————. "Annapolis." May 31, 1759. *Maryland Gazette* Collection, Archives of Maryland Online, MSA SC 2731. https://msa.maryland.gov/megafile/msa/speccol/sc4800/sc4872/001280/html/m1280-0130.html.

————. "Annapolis." July 19, 1759. *Maryland Gazette* Collection, Archives of Maryland Online, MSA SC 2731. https://msa.maryland.gov/megafile/msa/speccol/sc4800/sc4872/001280/html/m1280-0157.html.

————. "Annapolis." June 9, 1763. *Maryland Gazette* Collection, Archives of Maryland Online, MSA SC 2731. https://msa.maryland.gov/megafile/msa/speccol/sc4800/sc4872/001280/html/m1280-0985.html.

———. "Annapolis." April 18, 1765. *Maryland Gazette* Collection, Archives of Maryland Online, MSA SC 2731. https://msa.maryland.gov/megafile/msa/speccol/sc4800/sc4872/001280/html/m1280-1423.html.

———. "Annapolis." August 29, 1765. *Maryland Gazette* Collection, Archives of Maryland Online, MSA SC 2731. https://msa.maryland.gov/megafile/msa/speccol/sc4800/sc4872/001280/html/m1280-1511.html.

———. "Annapolis." December 10, 1765. *Maryland Gazette* Collection, Archives of Maryland Online, MSA SC 2731. https://msa.maryland.gov/megafile/msa/speccol/sc4800/sc4872/001280/html/m1280-1559.html.

Maryland Gazette. "The Speech of the Honourable Robert Dinwiddie, Esq. Lieutenant Governor, and Commander in Chief, of the Colony and Dominion of Virginia, to the General Assembly of the Said Province, on Thursday, the 1st of Day of November 1753." December 6, 1753. *Maryland Gazette* Collection, Archives of Maryland Online, https://msa.maryland.gov/megafile/msa/speccol/sc4800/sc4872/001279/html/m1279-0414.html.

McCardell, James. *Cunne Shote, the Indian Chief, a Great Warrior of the Cherokee Nation*. Print, c. 1750–99. Miriam and Ira D. Wallach Division of Art, Prints and Photographs: Print Collection, New York Public Library, New York Public Library Digital Collections. https://digitalcollections.nypl.org/items/510d47da-2450-a3d9-e040-e00a18064a99.

Pleasants, J. Hall, ed. *Proceedings and Acts of the General Assembly of Maryland 1752–1754*. Baltimore: Maryland Historical Society, 1933. https://msa.maryland.gov/megafile/msa/speccol/sc2900/sc2908/000001/000050/html/am50p--5.html.

———. "Proceedings of the Lower House." In *Archives of Maryland*. Vol. 52, *Proceedings of the General Assembly of Maryland 1755–1756*. Baltimore: Maryland Historical Society, 1935. https://msa.maryland.gov/megafile/msa/speccol/sc2900/sc2908/000001/000052/html/index.html.

———. "Proceedings of the Upper House." In *Archives of Maryland*. Vol. 50, *Proceedings and Acts of the General Assembly of Maryland 1752–1754*. Baltimore: Maryland Historical Society, 1933. https://msa.maryland.gov/megafile/msa/speccol/sc2900/sc2908/000001/000050/html/index.html

———. "Proceedings of the Upper House of Assembly." In *Archives of Maryland*. Vol. 55, *Proceedings and Acts of the General Assembly of Maryland 1757–1758*. Baltimore: Maryland Historical Society, 1938. https://msa.maryland.gov/megafile/msa/speccol/sc2900/sc2908/000001/000055/html/index.html.

———. "Proceedings of the Upper House." In *Archives of Maryland*. Vol. 56, *Proceedings and Acts of the General Assembly of Maryland 1758–1761*. Baltimore: Maryland Historical Society, 1939. https://msa.maryland.gov/megafile/msa/speccol/sc2900/sc2908/000001/000056/html/index.html.

Reynolds, Joshua Sir. *Sir Jeffery Amherst, Knight of the Most Honorabale Order of Bath*. Print, 1766. Library of Congress Prints and Photographs Division, Washington, D.C. https://www.loc.gov/item/2001696980/.

Rocque, John. "#16 Plan of Fort Ligonier." In *A Set of Plans and Forts in America: Reduced from Actual Surveys, 1765*. London: Mary Ann Rocque, 1765.

———. "#28 Plan of Fort Pitts-burgh." In *A Set of Plans and Forts in America: Reduced from Actual Surveys, 1765*. London: Mary Ann Rocque, 1765.

Sharpe, Horatio. "George Washington Papers, Series 4, General Correspondence: Horatio Sharpe to Cherokee Indians, 1756." 1756. Manuscript/mixed material, Library of Congress. https://www.loc.gov/item/mgw442499/.

Spillsbury, John. *A New Map of North America from the Latest Discoveries*. Map, c. 1763. Library of Congress, Miscellaneous Pamphlet Collection and American Imprint Collection. https://www.loc.gov/item/74695015/.

Tietz, Johann Ludwig. *Sixth and Last Lord Baltimore, Frederick Calvert (1731–1771)*. Oil on canvas, c. 1750–98.

Visit of Pontiac and the Indians to Major Gladwin. Drawing, c. 1760. Ohio History Connection Archives.

Washington, George. "George Washington's Map, Accompanying His 'Journal to the Ohio,' 1754." Library of Congress Geography and Map Division. https://www.loc.gov/item/99446116/

———. "Journey to the French Commandant: Narrative." Founders Online, National Archives. https://founders.archives.gov/documents/Washington/01-01-02-0003-0002.

Secondary Sources

Anderson, Fred. *Defeat of General Braddock: 9th July 1755*. Wood engraving, 1836. Library of Congress Prints and Photographs Division, Washington, D.C. www.loc.gov/item/2005685065/.

———. *The War That Made America: A Short History of the French and Indian War*. New York: Penguin Group, 2005.

Bailey, Kenneth P. *The Ohio Company of Virginia and the Westward Movement 1748–1792*. Glendale, CA: Arthur H. Clark Company, 1939.

Banvard, Joseph. *Tragic Scenes in the History of Maryland and the Old French War.* Boston: Gould and Lincoln, 1856.

Black, J. William. "Maryland's Attitude in the Struggle for Canada." In *Johns Hopkins University Study in Historical and Political Science.* Tenth series, vol. 7. Baltimore, MD: Johns Hopkins Press, 1892. https://archive.org/details/marylandsattitud00blac/mode/2up.

Borneman, Walter. *The French and Indian War: Deciding the Fate of North America.* New York: HarperCollins, 2006.

Burns, Albert S. *Fort Frederick, Hagerstown, Washington County, MD.* Photograph, 1933. Historic American Buildings Survey. https://www.loc.gov/item/md0835/.

Calloway, Colin G. *The Scratch of a Pen: 1763 and the Transformation of North America.* New York: Oxford University Press, 2006.

Crytzer, Brady J. *War in the Peaceable Kingdom: The Kittanning Raid of 1756.* Yardley, PA: Westholme Publishing, 2016.

Edgar, Lady. *A Colonial Governor in Maryland: Horatio Sharpe and His Times 1753–1773.* New York: Longmans, Green and Co., 1912.

Everstine, Carl N. "The Establishment of Legislative Power in Maryland." *Maryland Law Review* 12, no. 2 (Spring 1951): 99–121.

Ferling, John. *Almost a Miracle: The American Victory in the War of Independence.* New York: Oxford University Press, 2007.

Fowler, William M. *Empires at War: The French and Indian War and the Struggle for North America, 1754–1763.* New York: Walker & Company, 2005.

Hoffman, Ronald. *Princes of Ireland, Planters of Maryland: A Carroll Saga 1500–1782.* Chapel Hill: University of North Carolina Press, 2000.

The Indians Giving a Talk to Colonel Bouquet in a Conference at a Council Fire, Near His Camp on the Banks of the Muskingum in North America in Oct. 1764. Library of Congress Prints and Photographs Division, Washington, D.C. https://www.loc.gov/pictures/item/2003688819/.

Irving, Washington. *Horatio Sharpe, Governor of Maryland.* Miriam and Ira D. Wallach Division of Art, Prints and Photographs, Print Collection, New York Public Library, New York Public Library Digital Collections. https://digitalcollections.nypl.org/items/510d47da-f3ff-a3d9-e040-e00a18064a99.

Land, Aubrey C. *Colonial Maryland: A History.* Millwood, NY: KTO Press, 1981.

Lowdermilk, William. "Fort Cumberland, 1755." In *History of Cumberland (Maryland) from the Time of the Indian Town, Caiuctucuc, in 1728, up to the Present Day, Embracing an Account of Washington's First Campaign and Battle of Fort*

Necessity, Together with a History of Braddock's Campaign. Washington, D.C.: James Anglim, 1878.

Mayer, Francis Blackwell. *The Burning of the* Peggy Stewart. Oil on canvas, 1896. Collection of the Maryland State Archives, MSA SC 1545-1111.

McSherry, James. *A History of Maryland: From Its Settlement in 1634 to the Year 1848, with an Account of its First Discovery, and the Various Exploration of the Chesapeake Bay*. Baltimore, MD: J. Murphy & Company, 1852.

Morgan, Edmund S., and Helen M. Morgan. *The Stamp Act Crisis: Prologue to Revolution*. Chapel Hill: University of North Carolina Press, 1953.

Morgan, Ted. *Wilderness at Dawn: The Settling of the North American Continent*. New York: Simon and Schuster, 1993.

Morton, Joseph C. *The American Revolution*. Westport, CT: Greenwood Press, 2003.

Nye, Eric W. "Pounds Sterling to Dollars: Historical Conversion of Currency." August 1, 2020. https://www.uwyo.edu/numimage/currency.htm.

O'Meara, Walter. *Guns at the Forks*. Pittsburgh, PA: University of Pittsburgh Press, 1979.

Parkman, Francis. *Montcalm and Wolfe: The French and Indian War*. Boston: Little, Brown, and Company, 1897.

Powell, Allan. *Forgotten Heroes of the Maryland Frontier: Christopher Gist, Evan Shelby, Jr., Thomas Cresap*. Baltimore: Gateway Press, 2001.

———. *Maryland and the French and Indian War*. Baltimore: Gateway Press, 1998.

Ridout, Elizabeth. *Conjectural Drawing of the 2nd Maryland Statehouse*. Drawing. Collection of the Maryland State Archives, MSA SC 1444-1-2.

Sandham, Henry. *Founding of Maryland: Landing at St. Mary's, 1634*. Print, 1894. Miriam and Ira D. Wallach Division of Art, Prints and Photographs, Picture Collection, New York Public Library, New York Public Library Digital Collections. https://digitalcollections.nypl.org/items/510d47e0-f3ab-a3d9-e040-e00a18064a99.

Sartain, William. *Gen. Braddock*. Engraving, New York, c. 1899. Library of Congress Prints and Photographs Division, Washington, D.C. https://www.loc.gov/item/2014645011/.

Scharf, J. Thomas. *History of Western Maryland: Being a History of Frederick, Montgomery, Carroll, Washington, Allegany, and Garrett Counties from the Earliest Period to the Present Day*. Vol. 1. Baltimore: Regional Publishing Office, 1968.

The Stamp Act Denounced. Wood engraving, 1913. Library of Congress Prints and Photographs Division, Washington, D.C. www.loc.gov/item/2006679820/.

Ward, Matthew C. *Breaking the Backcountry: The Seven Years' War in Virginia and Pennsylvania, 1754–1765*. Pittsburgh, PA: University of Pittsburgh Press, 2003.

Waud, Alfred R. *Taking possession of Fort Duquesne*. Print, c. 1880. Miriam and Ira D. Wallach Division of Art, Prints and Photographs, Picture Collection, New York Public Library, New York Public Library Digital Collections. https://www.digitalcollections.nypl.org/items/510d47e0-f490-a3d9-e040-e00a18064a99

White, Bryant. *Cherokee Treaty at Fort Frederick*. Oil on canvas, 2012.

Wicker, Elmus. "Colonial Monetary Standards Contrasted: Evidence from the Seven Years' War." *Journal of Economic History* 45, no. 4 (December 1985): 869–84. https://www.jstor.org/stable/2121884.

INDEX

A

Abercromby, Major General James 69
Allegany Mountain 62
Amherst, Jeffery 75, 82
An Act for Granting a Supply of Forty
　Thousand Pounds for His Majesty's
　Service and Striking Thirty-Four
　Thousand and Fifteen Pounds Six
　Shillings Thereof in Bills of Credit,
　and Raising a Fund for Sinking the
　Same 49
An Act for His Majesty's Service 35
Annapolis 11, 34, 36, 40, 42, 43, 54,
　57, 58, 61, 85, 90, 91, 94, 96
Ark and the Dove 23

B

Battle of Bushy Run 88
Battle of the Monongahela 42
Beall, Captain Alexander 62
Belcher, Jonathan, governor of New
　Jersey 36
Braddock, General Edward 37

C

Calvert, Cecilius 22, 23, 25, 93
Calvert, Frederick 24, 26, 35, 40, 41,
　52, 54, 68, 69, 72, 80, 89
Campbell, John, Earl of Loudoun. *See*
　Loudoun
Carroll, Charles, of Carrollton 96
Carroll, Dr. Charles 30
Catawba 32, 46, 47
Céloron de Blainville, Captain Pierre-
　Joseph. *See* Céloron Expedition
Céloron expedition 16, 17, 18
Cherokee 32, 46, 47, 61, 62
Coercive Acts 96
Conococheague 50
Considerations 92
Cresap, Thomas 85
Croghan, George 16, 83

D

Darcy, Robert, Lord Holdernesse. *See*
　Lord Holdernesse
Delaware 14, 15, 19, 45, 62, 83, 88

Dinwiddie, Robert 20, 21, 22, 27, 31, 35, 48, 54
Dulaney, Daniel 33, 92
Duquesne, Sieur de Menneville 20

E

England 11, 14, 17, 18, 21, 22, 38, 42, 58

F

Forbes, Brigadier General John 70
Forks of the Ohio 18, 20, 33
Fort Bedford 75, 80
Fort Cumberland 42, 43, 52, 61, 64, 66, 67, 68, 74, 78, 85
Fort Detroit 85
Fort Duquesne 33, 36, 40, 42, 49, 53, 64, 72, 73, 74, 75
Fort Frederick 54, 56, 57, 59, 60, 61, 62, 64, 73, 74, 78, 80, 81, 85, 89
Fort Le Beouf 20, 21
Fort Ligonier 72, 75, 80
Fort Pitt 75, 82, 85, 88
France 11, 14, 16, 17, 21, 62, 80, 82, 83, 99
Frederick County 45, 47, 85, 88, 93
French 7, 8, 13, 14, 15, 16, 17, 18, 19, 20, 21, 22, 25, 26, 27, 29, 30, 31, 32, 33, 34, 35, 36, 37, 38, 39, 40, 42, 44, 45, 47, 50, 52, 56, 58, 62, 73, 74, 75, 80, 81, 82, 83, 88, 89, 98

G

Gist, Christopher 18, 20
governor's council 11, 24, 34, 38, 49, 50, 80, 81, 89
Great Britain 12, 17, 20, 22, 27, 29, 31, 35, 70, 77, 82, 83, 89, 90, 92, 93, 94, 95, 96, 98, 99

H

Hagerstown 98
Hamilton, James 17

Hammond, Phillip 54
Hood, Zachariah 91

I

Iroquois 14, 15, 19, 30, 31, 33, 82

J

Johnson, William 82, 83

L

Loudoun 57, 58, 59, 64, 66, 68, 69
lower house 7, 24, 26, 30, 31, 32, 33, 34, 35, 39, 40, 41, 44, 46, 47, 48, 49, 50, 53, 54, 56, 58, 59, 60, 61, 64, 67, 68, 69, 70, 71, 72, 73, 78, 79, 80, 89, 93, 94

M

Marquis de Vaudreuil 62
Maryland 11, 19, 21, 22, 23, 24, 26, 27, 29, 30, 31, 32, 33, 34, 35, 36, 37, 38, 39, 40, 42, 43, 44, 45, 46, 47, 48, 49, 50, 54, 55, 56, 57, 58, 59, 60, 61, 62, 64, 66, 67, 68, 69, 70, 71, 72, 73, 74, 75, 76, 77, 78, 79, 80, 81, 85, 86, 88, 89, 90, 92, 93, 94, 96, 98, 99, 106
Maryland Assembly 22, 23, 28, 29, 37, 49, 55, 57, 64, 74, 75, 76, 80, 94
Maryland Convention of 1774 96, 98
Maryland forces 60, 62, 68, 69, 72, 74, 82
Maryland Gazette 27, 29, 50, 85, 90, 92
Massachusetts 21, 29, 94, 96
militia 20, 35, 40, 42, 43, 45, 47, 50, 57, 59, 64, 68, 69, 70, 72, 78, 85, 98
Monongahela River 40
Murdock, William 54

N

Native Americans 40

New York 12, 14, 15, 16, 21, 29, 30, 31, 36, 46
North Mountain 50

O

Ohio Company 18, 19
Ohio Company of Virginia. *See* Ohio Company
Ohio Valley 14, 16, 17, 18, 19, 20, 22, 27, 29, 78, 82

P

Parliament 90, 92, 93, 94, 95, 96, 98
Peggy Stewart 96
Pennsylvania 12, 14, 15, 16, 17, 18, 19, 21, 27, 36, 38, 40, 42, 43, 47, 48, 50, 62, 70, 72, 80, 81, 85, 89
Plater, George 33
Pontiac 83, 89, 90
Prather, Thomas 85
Proclamation of 1763 90

R

Rideout, John 62
Riley, Lieutenant James 64
Robinson, Thomas 36, 38
Royal American 57

S

1758 56, 68, 69, 73, 74, 75, 90
1755 7, 37, 38, 40, 41, 42, 43, 45, 62
1754 7, 21, 27, 29, 30, 31, 33, 34, 36, 37, 44, 48, 60, 88
1759 75, 77, 78, 80, 82, 88
1756 41, 42, 44, 46, 52, 54, 55, 56, 59, 61, 62, 70, 71, 79, 89
1760 81, 82
1763 83, 85, 88, 90, 98
Sharpe, Horatio 11, 21, 22, 23, 24, 42, 60
Shawnee 19, 45, 62, 83, 85, 88
Shelby, Lieutenant Evan 62
Shirley, William 21, 29, 44, 48, 52

southern Indians. *See* Catawaba and Cherokee
Spain 11
Stamp Act 90, 92, 93, 94, 95
Stanwix, Colonel John 59
St. Clair, John 70
Stewart, Anthony 96
Stone, Thomas 98

T

Tasker, Benjamin 33, 54
Tea Act 95
Thomas, Phillip 54
Tilghman, Edward 54
Tilghman, Matthew 30, 33, 54
Townsend Acts 94, 95
Townsend, Charles 94
trade 13, 14, 15, 17, 18, 30, 82, 83, 96
Trent, Captain William 33

U

upper house 24, 34, 35, 38, 39, 40, 45, 49, 50, 52, 53, 54, 59, 60, 61, 67, 69, 70, 71, 72, 73, 77, 79, 80, 89, 92

V

Venango 20
Virginia 12, 17, 18, 19, 20, 21, 22, 27, 29, 30, 31, 32, 33, 34, 35, 38, 40, 42, 46, 48, 54, 57, 62, 64, 67, 70, 85, 89

W

Wahachy of Keeowee 62
Walking Purchase of 1737 14
Washington, George 20, 22, 27, 33
Will's Creek 19, 21, 29, 33, 36, 38
Winchester 62
Wolstenholme, Daniel 62

ABOUT THE AUTHOR

T im Ware grew up outside of Martinsburg, West Virginia, in a region filled with history spanning from the colonial period to the American Civil War and beyond. His passion for history pushed him to pursue an undergraduate degree in history from Shepherd University and a graduate degree in American history from American Public University. In his first book, Tim dives into Maryland's participation in a war that began as a skirmish on the frontiers of Pennsylvania and grew into a global war for empire. Tim resides in Hagerstown, Maryland, with his wife, Heather; son, Clyde; and two dogs, Nell and Kash.